JUNIOR ICE HOCKEY:

THE LEAGUES BEFORE THE LEAGUE

BY: DEREK SCHAEDIG

Junior Ice Hockey:
The Leagues Before The League

This is a work of nonfiction.
No names have been changed, no characters invented,
no events fabricated.

Cover photos by: Brandon Anderson
Edited by Amanda Karby
Proofread by Sharon AvRutick
Book Design by Veronica Scott

ISBN: 979-8-218-16918-3 (paperback)

To my coaches,
teammates,
billets,
the fans,
and my family

CONTENTS

A NOTE FROM THE AUTHOR

Now retired from the game, I was an ice hockey goalie for twenty years. Before heading off to play junior ice hockey, or "juniors," I was born and raised in the small town of Chelsea, Michigan. After playing for various local travel teams growing up, I competed for my high school program for four years before making the jump to the junior ranks at eighteen years old. I then played in both the North American Hockey League (NAHL) with the Janesville Jets and the United States Hockey League (USHL) with the Chicago Steel and the Lincoln Stars. After playing juniors for two years, I then moved on to play National Collegiate Athletic Association (NCAA) Division I ice hockey for Harvard University. It was in juniors, though, that I experienced some of the best times of my life, some of the most challenging, and everything in between.

My family and I knew very little about junior ice hockey before I started. Thankfully, we had a support system around us in the hockey community to help us navigate. I wrote this book for families, coaches, athletes, or junior hockey fans in similar situations. When I was trying to traverse juniors, there were not many tangible resources available to help. That's where this book comes in: to help you understand juniors by providing a broad overview of the various leagues, and by illustrating some of my experiences so you can be prepared for that next step in a player's hockey journey.

Although some of this book discusses what I found difficult in juniors, I am nevertheless extremely grateful for what playing junior ice hockey has given me. I never would have been able to achieve my lifelong dream of playing ice hockey at the Division I level or attend a university like Harvard without it. It is through juniors that I learned so much about hockey, myself, and life in general. Without a doubt, juniors made me the person I am today, and I carry the lessons I learned with me in my daily life.

Everything you'll read here is from my perspective, but there are a lot of leagues, teams, and players out there; some may not have had the same experiences I had, and others may disagree with what I describe. As you read on, I encourage you to keep in mind I am not representative of all player experiences, but I hope my journey will help explain junior hockey to those who haven't experienced it before from an insider's perspective.

CHAPTER ONE:
WELCOME TO JUNIORS

It was mid-December of 2016. The Saturday before that life-changing week, my junior ice hockey team, the Janesville Jets, took on one of our division rivals: the Springfield Junior Blues. As a goalie, I earned the starting position for the second night in a row after a win the game before. I was confident. *No one is scoring on me tonight,* I thought.

But as many goalies know, that's not always how hockey works. On that Saturday, I gave up three goals on nineteen shots, leaving me with a less-than-ideal .842 save percentage for the night. Thirty-two minutes into the game, I was yanked from the net due to my poor performance, and my night in goal was over.

Just as I was getting ready for practice the following week, my head coach called me into his office—the equivalent of getting called into the principal's office when you know you're in big trouble. In this case, the trouble was playing one of my worst games of the season thus far, and the consequences were typically far from a slap on the wrist. I awaited the inevitable. Either I was getting traded to another franchise or, worse yet, cut from my team altogether. I pictured myself saying goodbye to my coaches, my teammates, and my host family. As my anxiety grew, my chest tightened. I prepared my speech: "I appreciate the opportunity, coach. Thanks for giving me a shot."

At age 18, I traipsed into my coach's office and took a seat. He sat opposite me, not even the slightest glimmer of expression on his face. *He's have to had done this a hundred times.* I contemplated as my thoughts began to swirl. *I guess there's no room for emotion in juniors.*

After what felt like an eternity, he finally spoke. "Derek, Lincoln called. They need a goalie for the next two weeks. I don't know if you'll play or not, but they need to know now or they're moving on to someone else."

I sat there, shook like a deer just after evading a semi-truck. Based in Nebraska's capital, the Lincoln Stars compete in the highest level of junior ice hockey in the United States. I wasn't being cut—I was getting a promotion.

Two weeks later, my new team and I had won all four games since I had been called up. On the last day of my tenure with the Stars in 2016, we celebrated a win against the Omaha Lancers, our fiercest rivals. After one of my first games, I was named one of the stars of the game. I found myself skating around the Ice Box, our home arena, a T-shirt in-hand, trying to decide which one of the three thousand fans in attendance that night to throw it to. Just two weeks after getting called into my coach's office expecting the worst, I was named Co-goaltender of the Week in the top junior league in the country. After a slow start to the first half of the season, I was back on scouts' radars and on my way to accomplishing my dream of earning a Division I hockey commitment. *What a ride*, I thought as I sat in my stall in shock after the game, unable to contain the smile on my face. *Welcome to juniors.*

***

Welcome to this book, and welcome to the wild world of junior ice hockey. I wrote this book to help families, coaches, young athletes, and junior hockey fans gain more knowledge of the sport and leagues in North America. Neither of my parents have ever played juniors, were recruited or participated in collegiate athletics, or have ever even played ice hockey. The junior hockey experience was a new one both for me and my family. Navigating juniors can be daunting, but this book will help you learn more about what it is and what to expect from the experience.

CHAPTER TWO

WHAT IS JUNIOR ICE HOCKEY, ANYWAY?

On November 27, 1890, a meeting took place that would transform the game of ice hockey forever. Thirteen men assembled at the Queen's Hotel in Toronto, Ontario, with a goal in mind: to "bring some order to the game" of the booming sport in eastern Canada.[1] At the time, hockey in Canada had little organization. They wanted to change that.

In that meeting, an early governing body of the sport named the Ontario Hockey Association (OHA) was born. In addition to establishing the preliminary rules of the game, the men instituted the "senior" series. Senior hockey is composed of teams around Canada and was an organized level in which the best players in the area could

---

1   Scott Young, *100 Years of Dropping the Puck: A History of the OHA* (Toronto: McClelland & Stewart, 1989).

compete. However, those who lacked the talent to play in these leagues were quickly left behind. Two years later, in 1892, the OHA created the "junior" category as well (also known as "juniors" colloquially). At first, juniors was simply a level below the senior leagues for the players who were not as talented as those in the higher ranks. But in the OHA's annual meeting in early December 1897, the association made a rule change to juniors that has stuck ever since: only players under twenty years old would be able to compete. Now, senior hockey is less popular, and juniors has risen immensely in its prominence and is often the focus of many young hockey players.

So, what is juniors today? A system of competitive, developmental leagues designed for players looking to advance to the next level of their career, whether at the collegiate or professional levels. As simple as that may sound, there are a lot of leagues out there, and each is different in its own way. Because there are so many in North America, determining which are better than others can be a challenge. As such, this section does not necessarily rank all leagues in order, but instead provides a broad overview of each league and the junior hockey system so you have a better understanding of the available options. Additionally, the leagues themselves change over time, so it is important to research current details of each league for the most up-to-date information.

WHO CAN PLAY IN JUNIORS?

Juniors is typically for players of ages sixteen to twenty.[2] According to the most recent USA Hockey Annual Guide available, the system is designed for "athletes who are at least 16 years of age and no older than 20 as of the 31st day of December of the current season of competition."[3] This means that players can be twenty-one years old and actively in juniors as long as they turn twenty-one after December 31 of their current season. These players, in their last year of being able to compete in juniors, are commonly referred to as "age-outs." Because juniors is a developmental system, leagues have varying rules in place regarding how many age-outs teams can have. For

---

2   There are some exceptions to the sixteen-year-old entry age requirement. The Canadian Hockey League allows a very select few fifteen-year-olds to compete in juniors through being granted "exceptional player status." According to a press release by the Western Hockey League, "exceptional player status is granted to a player whose qualities not only on the ice, but as a person, deem the player deserving of the rare privilege of participating in the Canadian Hockey League (CHL) at an early age." https://whl.ca/article/bc-hockey-announces-exceptional-player-status-for-connor-bedard

3   USA Hockey, USA Hockey 2022–23 Annual Guide, 2022.

example: the United States Hockey League (USHL), the top junior hockey league in the United States, allows each team to have four age-out players on their active rosters during the majority of the regular season.

Since junior hockey leagues in North America want to develop players close to home, there are also limitations on the number of players outside of the league's home country that are allowed to compete in that league. Players who are citizens of countries other than their league's home country are typically called "import players," or "imports." This means if an athlete is a European citizen playing in a North American league, they are considered an import. As of 2023, in the USHL, teams are allowed to have four import players on their rosters.[4]

Have I lost you yet with all these rules? There are a lot, and there are many intricacies and exceptions, as well, all of which can affect an athlete's decision to play in certain leagues. Since each league does have its own set of rules, it's important to check with the coach, scout, or advisor

---

4   Michael Caples, "USHL Announces Rule Changes for 2017–18 Season," MiHockey (blog), January 24, 2017, http://mihockey.com/2017/01/ ushl-announces-rule-changes-for-2017-18-season/.

you are communicating with when trying to select a team to play for. For more information on advisors, refer to the "Advisors" section in Chapter Three: "Be a true pro."

When researching teams and leagues, there are a number of things to consider: level of play, costs, advancement opportunities, compatibility with coaching staff, and travel schedules, among others. Below is a list of many of the junior hockey leagues in both Canada and the US. This list is intended to provide a brief overview of information, but it is not meant to be comprehensive. Athletes and their families should always research leagues and teams before they commit to playing. To research a program, you can visit a team's website, ask around your own hockey network, or reach out to an advisor to help.

THE LEAGUES

LEAGUES IN THE UNITED STATES OF AMERICA

In the United States, junior hockey is divided into three tiers: I, II, and III. These tiers reflect the level of play, Tier I being the most prolific in advancing players to the NCAA or professional ranks. USA Hockey, the governing body of hockey in the United States, oversees some, but not all, of these leagues.

Tier I: United States Hockey League (USHL)

- Advancement Opportunities[5] (for the following season):
  - o Professional franchises
  - o NCAA Division I
  - o Other junior leagues
- Costs:
  - o Training: Free
  - o Equipment: Free
  - o Housing: Free
  - o In this league, players live in host families' houses, referred to as "billet families" or "billets" (More information about billet families can be found in "Chapter Four: Life as a Junior Hockey Player").

---

5   The "Advancement Opportunities" section is based on where the majority of players compete the following year, but there are many routes players may take in their career.

- **League Information:**[6]

  o Sanctioned by USA Hockey.
  o Although there were precursors, the USHL as hockey fans know it today was founded in 1979.
  o As of the 2022–23 season, the USHL is home to sixteen teams located throughout the Midwest.
  o In the 2018–19 regular season, the USHL averaged 2,344 fans per game.[7]

Tier II:
North American Hockey League (NAHL)

- **Advancement Opportunities:**

  o NCAA Division I
  o NCAA Division III
  o Other junior leagues

- **Costs:**

  o Training: Free
  o Equipment: Teams provide sticks, helmet, gloves, and pants, but players purchase the rest of their gear with some discounts.
  o Housing: Hundreds of dollars per month (billets).

---

6   United States Hockey League, "Clark Cup;" and HockeyDB.com, "USHL 2018–19 Team Attendance."

7   The attendance statistics mentioned above are based on the most recent figures as of February 2023 for regular seasons in each league not affected by the COVID-19 pandemic.

- **League Information:**[8]
  - o Sanctioned by USA Hockey.
  - o Founded in 1975.
  - o As of the 2022–23 season, the NAHL is home to twenty-nine teams located throughout the United States.
  - o In the 2018–19 regular season, the NAHL averaged 1,207 fans per game.

United States Premier Hockey League (USPHL)

The USPHL is a bit different than the rest of the junior leagues in the United States for a couple of reasons. First, there are multiple levels under the USPHL umbrella:

1. The National Collegiate Development Conference (NCDC) (Tier II)
2. Premier (Tier III)
3. Elite (Tier III)
4. Midget

To get a better understanding of the USPHL, let's take a look at one of its franchises: the New Jersey Hitmen. The Hitmen have many teams within the organization, and their team members could be playing for one of four levels

---

8   North American Hockey League, "NAHL History;" and HockeyDB.com, "NAHL 2018–19 Team Attendance.

and still be playing for the Hitmen franchise. The first three levels (NCDC, Premier, and Elite) are different levels of junior leagues, while the Midget level is one designated for youth player development. Additionally, just as players can be traded or loaned up and down to different-level junior leagues at any time, the same goes for the USPHL—players can move up from the Premier level to the NCDC, for example. So, if a coach ever contacts you and says they are a part of the USPHL, your first question should be, "Which level is the team?"

Another reason the USPHL is a bit different from the other US leagues is that, in 2016, it applied to be granted Tier II status by USA Hockey. This would have made it so that players competing in the USPHL would not have to pay to play hockey, like the rest of Tier III junior hockey competitors (although players in the NCDC would still have to pay for housing). That motion was ultimately denied by USA Hockey.[9] However, most consider the NCDC level to be Tier II level with the Premier and Elite divisions being Tier III. With many college and professional alumni from the USPHL, the debate rages on over how the USPHL compares to other junior leagues.

---

9   The Junior Hockey News, "USPHL Denied Tier II Status By USA Hockey Junior Council – And What's Next."

Nevertheless, many teams, especially in the NCDC level, have great advancement opportunities.

USPHL NCDC

- **Advancement Opportunities:**
  - o Many NCAA Division I
  - o NCAA Division III
  - o Other junior leagues

- **Costs:**
  - o Training: Despite USA Hockey's ruling, the NCDC no longer requires players to pay to play; however, all other USPHL levels still require fees to play for their programs.
  - o Equipment: Teams provide sticks, helmet, gloves, and pants, but players purchase the rest of their gear with some discounts.
  - o Housing: Hundreds of dollars per month (either apartments, houses, or billets).

- **League Information:**[10]
  - o Not sanctioned by USA Hockey.
  - o Founded in 2012.
  - o As of the 2022–23 season, the NCDC level of the USPHL is home to fourteen teams in the

---

10   United States Premier Hockey League, "About/History of the USPHL."

Northeastern US (but the USPHL as a whole extends
throughout the US).

o Numbers vary by level, but overall fan attendance in
the USPHL is much lower than both the USHL and
NAHL separately.

Tier III: "Pay-to-play"[11]

Unlike tiers I and II, tier III consists of many "pay-to-play"
leagues. This means that gear and housing are not
covered, and families can expect to pay the team to cover
costs such as travel, ice bills, and other team expenses. The
fees families pay have a wide range but are typically in the
ballpark of a few thousand all the way up to $10,000 or
more.

---

11   For the US Tier III, Major Junior, and Junior A levels, these leagues
are listed in alphabetical order since it can be difficult to compare their
competition levels. Refer to the "Advancement Opportunities" sections
under each league for more information on the level of play usually
associated with each league.

Eastern Hockey League (EHL)

- Advancement Opportunities:
  - NCAA Division III
  - American Collegiate Hockey Association (ACHA) programs (commonly referred to as "club" collegiate athletics)
    - Just like the NCAA, club programs have different levels as well. Teams can either be members of the ACHA Division I, II, or III levels.
  - Other junior leagues
- Costs:
  - Training: Thousands of dollars per year.
  - Equipment: Teams provide sticks, helmet, gloves, and pants, but players purchase the rest of their gear with some discounts.
  - Housing: Hundreds of dollars per month (either apartments, houses, or billets).

- **League Information:**[12]

  o Not sanctioned by USA Hockey.

  o Founded in 2014.

  o As of the 2022–23 season, the EHL is home to nineteen teams in the Northeastern US.

  o In the 2014–15 season, the EHL averaged 102 fans per game.

  o Unlike the USHL and the NAHL, the Eastern Hockey League is split into two levels: the EHL and the EHL Premier, the latter being its developmental league.

North American 3 Hockey League (NA3HL)

- **Advancement Opportunities:**

  o NCAA Division III

  o ACHA

  o Other junior leagues

- **Cost:**

  o Training: Thousands of dollars per year.

  o Equipment: Player provided.

  o Housing: Hundreds of dollars per month (either apartments, houses, or billets).

---

12   Eastern Hockey League (EHL), "All-Time EHL Records" and "EHL Teams;" and Pointstreak Sports Technologies, "Eastern Hockey League 2014–15 Fan Attendance."

- League Information:[13]
  - Sanctioned by USA Hockey.
  - Founded in 2010.
  - As of the 2022–23 season, the NA3HL is home to thirty-four teams located throughout the United States.
  - In the 2018–19 regular season, the NA3HL averaged 320 fans per game.

LEAGUES IN CANADA

Canada has four junior hockey levels. Ranked in order of level of play, they are as follows:

1. Major Junior
2. Junior A
3. Junior B
4. Junior C

Major Junior: Canadian Hockey League (CHL)

Founded in 1975, the CHL is the umbrella organization for three leagues under it: the Western Hockey League ("the Dub"), the Ontario Hockey League ("the O"), and the Quebec Major Junior Hockey league ("the Q"). Major

---

13   North American Tier III Hockey League (NA3HL), "About," "Teams," and "NA3HL Game Center 2018–19 Fan Attendance."

junior players are paid a stipend to compete for their programs; as such, they are not eligible to play NCAA hockey since they are technically considered professional athletes. Therefore, the goal of many of these young players is to make it to the National Hockey League (known as making it to "The League" by hockey communities alike).

The CHL knows how to produce NHL players. In fact, the CHL produces the most NHL players of all the junior hockey leagues in existence today.[14] Playing for one of these highly touted franchises is a dream come true for many young players in North America. Every year, these three major junior leagues compete for one of the most popular tournaments in Canada: the Memorial Cup. Winning this trophy dubs the champion team as that year's best junior hockey franchise in Canada.

Ontario Hockey League (OHL)

- Advancement Opportunities:
  - Professional leagues
  - Canadian collegiate athletics (USPORTS)
  - Other junior leagues

---

14   Jason Bukala, "Scout's Analysis: Comparing How Leagues around the World Develop NHL Prospects."

- Costs:

  o Training: Free and players are provided with a stipend for summer training expenses.

  o Equipment: Free

  o Housing: Free (billets)

  o Education Package: The OHL, like all members of the CHL, cover educational expenses for players both while they are members in the CHL, and after they leave the CHL at a school of their choice for each year they competed in the CHL.[15]

- League Information:[16]

  o Sanctioned by Hockey Canada.

  o Although there were precursors, the OHL as it is known today began in 1980.

  o As of the 2022–23 season, the OHL is home to twenty teams located throughout Ontario, Michigan, and Pennsylvania.

  o In the 2018–19 season, the OHL averaged 3,944 fans per game.

---

15   The educational package a player receives as a member of the CHL is based on the educational costs associated with the closest post-secondary institution to the player's home address.

16   Ontario Hockey League, "Teams – Ontario Hockey League;" and HockeyDB.com, "Ontario Hockey League [1892–2023] History and Statistics" and "OHL 2018–19 Team Attendance."

Quebec Major Junior Hockey League (QMJHL)

- **Advancement Opportunities:**
  - Professional leagues
  - USPORTS
  - Other junior leagues

- **Costs:**
  - Training: Free and players are provided with a stipend for summer training expenses.
  - Equipment: Free
  - Housing: Free (billets)
  - Education Package: The QMJHL, like all members of the CHL, cover educational expenses for players both while they are members in the CHL, and after they leave the CHL at a school of their choice for each year they competed in the CHL.

- **League Information:**[17]
  - Sanctioned by Hockey Canada.
  - Founded in 1969.
  - As of the 2022–23 season, the QMJHL has eighteen teams located throughout Canadian provinces

---

17   Quebec Major Junior Hockey League, "History of the League" and "LHJMQ Standings;" and HockeyDB.com, "QMJHL 2018–19 Team Attendance."

Quebec, Nova Scotia, New Brunswick, and Prince Edward Island.

o In the 2018–19 season, the QMJHL averaged 3,305 fans per game.

Western Hockey League (WHL)

- Advancement Opportunities:

  o Professional leagues
  o USPORTS
  o Other junior leagues

- Costs:

  o Training: Free and players are provided with a stipend for summer training expenses.
  o Equipment: Free
  o Housing: Free (billets)
  o Education Package: The WHL, like all members of the CHL, cover educational expenses for players both while they are members in the CHL, and after they leave the CHL at a school of their choice for each year they competed in the CHL.

- **League Information:**[18]

  o Sanctioned by Hockey Canada.

  o Founded in 1966.

  o As of the 2022–23 season, the WHL is home to twenty-two teams located throughout western Canada and the US Pacific Northwest.

  o In the 2018–19 season, the WHL averaged 4,361 fans per game.

Junior A: Canadian Junior Hockey League (CJHL)

Just as the CHL is the umbrella organization for major junior with three member leagues below it, the CJHL is the umbrella organization for the many Junior A leagues in Canada. Unlike the CHL leagues wherein players are paid, players in Junior A leagues are unpaid and therefore still considered amateurs, which maintains their ability to play NCAA collegiate athletics. It's important to note that not all Junior A leagues or teams are created equal: since so many fall under this Junior A categorization, the levels of play and advancement opportunities vary greatly. Additionally, similar to how the CHL leagues compete for the Memorial Cup, these leagues compete for the

---

18   Western Hockey League, "About the WHL" and "WHL Teams & Directory – WHL Network;" and HockeyDB.com, "WHL 2018–19 Team Attendance."

Centennial Cup in order to be known as the year's best Canadian Junior A program.

Alberta Junior Hockey League (AJHL)

- **Advancement Opportunities:**
  - NCAA Division I
  - Some NCAA Division III
  - USPORTS
  - Other junior leagues

- **Costs:**
  - Training, equipment, and housing: Varies from team to team (billets).

- **League Information:**[19]
  - Sanctioned by Hockey Canada.
  - Founded in 1964.
  - As of the 2022–23 season, the AJHL is home to sixteen teams located throughout Alberta, Canada.
  - In the 2017–18 regular season, the AJHL averaged 718 fans per game.

---

19   Alberta Junior Hockey League, "AJHL History;" and HockeyDB. com, "AJHL 2017–18 Team Attendance."

Central Canada Hockey League (CCHL)

- **Advancement Opportunities:**

  o NCAA Division I
  o NCAA Division III
  o ACHA
  o USPORTS
  o Other junior leagues

- **Costs:**

  o Training: Thousands of dollars per year.
  o Equipment: Player provided.
  o Housing: Hundreds of dollars per month (billets).

- **League Information:**[20]

  o Sanctioned by Hockey Canada.
  o Founded in 1961.
  o As of the 2022–23 season, the CCHL is home to twelve teams located throughout Eastern Ontario, Canada.
  o In the 2018–19 season, the CCHL averaged 334 fans per game.

20　Central Canada Hockey League, "About the CCHL;" and HockeyDB.com, "CCHL 2018–19 Team Attendance."

Manitoba Junior Hockey League (MJHL)

- **Advancement Opportunities:**

  o Some NCAA Division I
  o NCAA Division III
  o ACHA
  o USPORTS
  o Other junior leagues

- **Costs:**

  o Training: There is a league fee of a few hundred dollars. Some teams in this league are pay-to-play, and some are not.
  o Equipment: Included in league fees and other fees from teams.
  o Housing: Hundreds of dollars per month (billets).

- **League Information:**[21]

  o Sanctioned by Hockey Canada.
  o Founded in 1917 as the Winnipeg & District Junior Hockey League, later renamed to the MJHL in 1933.
  o As of the 2022–23 season, the MJHL is home to twelve teams located in Manitoba, Canada.
  o In the 2018–19 season, the MJHL averaged 520 fans per game.

---

21   Manitoba Junior Hockey League, "MJHL History;" and HockeyDB.com, "MJHL 2018–19 Team Attendance."

Maritime Junior Hockey League (MHL)

- **Advancement Opportunities:**
  - NCAA Division III
  - ACHA
  - USPORTS
  - Other junior leagues

- **Costs:**
  - Training, equipment, and housing: A fee of a few thousand dollars covers all expenses (billets).

- **League Information:**[22]
  - Sanctioned by Hockey Canada.
  - Founded in 1967.
  - As of the 2022–23 season, the MHL is home to twelve teams located throughout the Canadian provinces of New Brunswick, Prince Edward Island, and Nova Scotia.
  - In the 2018–19 season, the MHL averaged 976 fans per game.

---

22 Maritime Junior Hockey League, "History of the MHL" and "MHL League Directory;" and HockeyDB.com, "MHL 2018–19 Team Attendance."

Northern Ontario Junior Hockey League (NOJHL)

- **Advancement Opportunities:**

  o Some NCAA Division I
  o NCAA Division III
  o ACHA
  o USPORTS
  o Other junior leagues

- **Costs:**

  o Training: Thousands of dollars per year.
  o Equipment: Player provided.
  o Housing: Hundreds of dollars per month (billets).

- **League Information:**[23]

  o Sanctioned by Hockey Canada.
  o Founded in 1962.
  o As of the 2022–23 season, the NOJHL is home to twelve teams located throughout Ontario and Michigan.
  o In the 2018–19 season, the NOJHL averaged 384 fans per game.

---

23 Northern Ontario Junior Hockey League. "About the NOJHL," and HockeyDB.com, "NOJHL 2018–19 Team Attendance."

Ontario Junior Hockey league (OJHL)

- **Advancement Opportunities:**

  o NCAA Division I
  o NCAA Division III
  o ACHA
  o USPORTS
  o Other junior leagues

- **Costs:**

  o Training, equipment, and housing: Varies from team to team (billets).

- **League Information:**[24]

  o Sanctioned by Hockey Canada and the OHA.
  o Founded in 1993.
  o As of the 2022–23 season, the OJHL is home to twenty-one teams located throughout Ontario and New York.
  o In the 2018–19 season, the OJHL averaged 220 fans per game.

---

24   HockeyDB.com, "Ontario Junior Hockey League History and Statistics" and "OJHL 2018–19 Team Attendance;" and Pointstreak Sports Technologies, "Home of the OJHL."

Quebec Junior Hockey League (Q JHL)

- Advancement Opportunities:

  o NCAA Division I
  o NCAA Division III
  o ACHA
  o USPORTS
  o Other junior leagues

- Costs:

  o Training and equipment: Thousands of dollars per year.
  o Housing: Most players live at home, but some live with billets.

- League Information:

  o Sanctioned by Hockey Canada.
  o Although previously under a different name, the Q JHL as a league was founded in 1988.
  o As of the 2022–23 season, the Q JHL is home to 13 teams located across Quebec, Canada.
  o In the 2018-19 season, the Q JHL averaged 1,375 fans per game.

Saskatchewan Junior Hockey League (SJHL)

- **Advancement Opportunities:**

  - Some NCAA Division I
  - NCAA Division III
  - ACHA
  - USPORTS
  - Other junior leagues

- **Costs:**

  - Training: Free
  - Equipment: All equipment but skates is covered by the league.
  - Housing: Free (billets)

- **League Information:**[25]

  - Sanctioned by Hockey Canada.
  - Founded in 1968.
  - As of the 2022–23 season, the SJHL is home to twelve teams located in Saskatchewan, Canada.
  - In the 2018–19 season, the SJHL averaged 735 fans per game.

---

25   Saskatchewan Junior Hockey League, "SJHL Historical Statistics" and "SJHL League Directory;" and HockeyDB.com, "SIJHL 2018–19 Team Attendance."

Superior International Junior Hockey League (SIJHL)

- **Advancement Opportunities:**
  - o NCAA Division III
  - o ACHA
  - o USPORTS
  - o Other junior leagues
- **Costs:**
  - o Training: Thousands of dollars per year.
  - o Equipment: Teams provide sticks, helmet, gloves, and pants, but players purchase the rest of their gear with some discounts.
  - o Housing: Hundreds of dollars per month (billets).
- **League Information:**[26]
  - o Sanctioned by Hockey Canada.
  - o Founded in 2001.
  - o As of the 2022–23 season, the SIJHL is home to seven teams located throughout Ontario, Minnesota, and Wisconsin.
  - o In the 2018–19 season, the SIJHL averaged 316 fans per game.

---

26   Superior International Junior Hockey League, "SIJHL History" and "SIJHL Member Clubs;" and HockeyDB.com, "SIJHL 2018–19 Team Attendance."

Junior A Outside of the CJHL

British Columbia Hockey League (BCHL): Despite being a successful junior league and member of the CJHL since 1993, the BCHL recently withdrew from the CJHL, which is the only Junior A hockey league sanctioned by Hockey Canada. The BCHL now functions on its own and no longer competes for the Centennial Cup among the other top junior leagues in Canada.

- **Advancement Opportunities:**
  - o NCAA Division I
  - o Some USPORTS
  - o Other junior leagues

- **Costs:**
  - o Training: Free
  - o Equipment: Free
  - o Housing: Free (billets)

- **League Information:**[27]
  - o Not sanctioned by Hockey Canada.
  - o Originally called the Okanagan-Mainline Junior Hockey League, the BCHL was founded in 1961.
  - o As of the 2022–23 season, the BCHL is home to eighteen teams located in British Columbia, Canada, and the US Pacific Northwest.
  - o In the 2018–19 season, the BCHL averaged 1,266 fans per game.

Junior B and C

These lower leagues are typically thought of as developmental programs for the Junior A ranks. There are many teams in these leagues as well, and as with all other leagues, it is important to do your research before an athlete decides to play at the Junior B and C levels.

---

27   British Columbia Junior Hockey League, "BCHL History;" and HockeyDB.com, "BCHL 2018–19 Team Attendance."

WOMEN'S JUNIOR ICE HOCKEY

Junior Women's Hockey League (JWHL)

For a long time, junior ice hockey was only established for men. However, in 2007, the JWHL was formed which made space for women to play junior ice hockey as well. Furthermore, recently there have been women playing in men's junior ice hockey leagues as well. Although progress has been made in equal opportunity for women's ice hockey, we still have a long way to go as an ice hockey community.

- **Advancement Opportunities:**
  - NCAA Division I
  - NCAA Division III
  - USPORTS

- **Costs:**
  - Training: Varies per team.
  - Equipment: Varies per team, but most teams provide helmet, gloves, and pants, while players purchase the rest of their gear with some discounts.
  - Housing: Some players live at home, some live at boarding schools, and some live with billets for hundreds of dollars per month.

- **League Information:**
  - o Not sanctioned.
  - o The JWHL was founded in 2007.
  - o As of the 2022–23 season, the JWHL is home to 7 teams in its U19 division located throughout the U.S. and Canada.
  - o In the 2018–19 season, the JWHL did not track fan attendance because they play at neutral sites. However, the league live streams 20,000+ viewers per weekend.

HOW TO BREAK INTO THESE LEAGUES

Almost every player, whether drafted or tendered (covered in Chapter Three), must attend tryout camps to make a junior hockey team. Young players may receive emails from junior programs inviting them to participate in their tryout camps, which take place at various times throughout the year and typically host large groups of players. Before committing to a camp, athletes should consider the type of camp, the team information provided by junior coaches and scouts, and the player retention rate from the previous year.

There are two types of tryout camps for junior hockey teams: pre-draft and main. Pre-draft camps, per their name, take place weeks before the league's draft. This type of camp typically fills up on a first come, first served basis, and any player who pays the fee can join. Pre-draft camps are what the majority of young players contacted by junior programs are probably invited to. They can be quite large, sometimes making it challenging for players to get noticed, so attend with caution—but any time players are competing in front of coaching staff or scouts is an opportunity to earn a spot on a roster.

Main camp, the second type of tryout camp, takes place after the league's draft. These camps are exclusively for a team's draft picks, tenders, and invitees. After completion, selected players are invited back for preseason, one step closer to making the team; after a few weeks of preseason and some more cuts, the initial roster is set.

But how do players get to these leagues in the first place? There are many different programs to play for in youth hockey. In Minnesota, many players come from high school programs; others come from AAA teams; others, especially in the Northeast, come from preparatory schools. Players have many different paths to get to juniors, and these paths foster different levels of exposure to be noticed by scouts and coaches. While it is important to be sure that young players be given opportunities to be seen, I'm a firm believer that their main focus should be their performance on the ice, and more importantly, their development both as an athlete and as a person.

The secret to making a junior team is that there is no secret. Junior owners, general managers, coaches, and scouts need their teams to win to stay employed—their livelihood rests on the performance of twenty or so teenagers. Therefore, for the most part, they are going to pick the player they believe gives them the best chance to make their hockey club successful. Rather than expending lots of time, energy, and money trying to get in front of every junior coach and scout out there, players should put most of their energy into becoming the best person and player they can be so that when they do get those opportunities, they're ready and able to perform at a high level.

One of the most overlooked ways to make a junior team is simple: be a decent human being. That doesn't mean a player has to be the nicest, or the coolest, or a perfect person by any means—they just have to try to be a good one.

Junior coaches and scouts make their own assessment of a player's on-ice attributes when they watch the individual compete. Typically, when they call a player's coach, they're not asking about their skills on the ice— they want to know what type of kid they are off the ice. Are they a team player? Do they work hard? Are they coachable? Can they fit in the locker room? If any of the answers to these questions are "no," that junior coach or scout is likely to move on to the next player—after all, they have hundreds of other players who would love to make their team. Besides focusing on developing an individual's game, trying to be a good person is another important way to crack a junior roster.

CHAPTER THREE:
"BE A TRUE PRO"

Although I played most of my second year of juniors in
Lincoln, I began the year with the Chicago Steel in the
USHL. They reserved my rights in the USHL draft while I
was still playing for the Janesville Jets in the NAHL.
During my short tenure with the Steel, my head coach
routinely preached a saying to us: "Be a true pro." By this,
he meant we were both to be treated like professionals
and to act as such, despite us not receiving pay in order to
maintain our amateur status and NCAA eligibility. We
were expected to be on time, to take responsibility for our
roles on the team, to give our best effort every day, to be a
good teammate, and to act in a professional manner both
on and off the ice. I had heard the importance of all of
these things separately growing up, but it wasn't until I
got to juniors that I fully understood what it really meant
to be a true pro.

"THE LEAGUE" DRAFT SYSTEM

In football, the draft system usually works like this:
players in college (or sometimes high school) declare

themselves eligible for the National Football League (NFL) draft that year, they are selected by a team, and in the following year, they're wearing that team's jersey.

Hockey, on the other hand, does not work this way. The National Hockey League (NHL) draft takes places in late June, and players do not need to declare themselves to be eligible. The thirty-two franchises in "The League" take turns over seven rounds drafting players from ages eighteen to twenty (non-North American players over twenty are eligible as well).[28] In most cases, however, these selected players do not suit up for that NHL club the following year. Being drafted simply means the franchise owns a player's rights for the following two years, or for NCAA players, thirty days after a player has left their college program.[29] Simply put, being drafted is just "dibs" on a player for a number of years; it does not mean they are necessarily going to be on an NHL team any time soon— or potentially ever. After players are drafted, they return to their college, or yes, their junior teams. This means some players in juniors are already drafted by NHL

---

28   Kristyn Repke, "NHL Draft 101: Rules and Information." NHL. com, June 29, 2013. https://www.nhl.com/bluejackets/news/ nhl-draft-101-rules-and-information/c-675546.

29   Repke, "NHL Draft 101: Rules and Information."

franchises, but they still compete for their junior programs.[30]

Many times, players who were drafted to The League while in juniors go on to play for several years in different programs before they sign their first professional contract. Once they do, they're typically still not on that NHL team's starting lineup just yet. There are five levels of professional hockey in the United States, listed in descending order by level of play:

1. The NHL
2. The American Hockey League (AHL)
3. The East Coast Hockey League (ECHL)
4. The Southern Professional Hockey League (SPHL)
5. The Federal Prospects Hockey League (FPHL)

Players who have been drafted by an NHL franchise and sign a professional contract end up in one of these leagues to develop their game further before making the jump to the NHL. This process can take years before a player gets

---

30 College commitments are similar to the NHL draft system in that players in juniors are many times committed to college programs for years before they move on to college. For example, I committed to play for Harvard University in my first year of juniors, but I also played a second year of juniors because Harvard did not have a spot for me on the roster yet.

their shot at playing a professional game, and for some, it may never come.

THE JUNIOR DRAFT SYSTEM

To begin, many junior hockey leagues have drafts somewhat similar to the NHL's system. In junior league drafts, teams take turns alternating reserving the rights of young players, and these players do not need to declare themselves to be eligible for these drafts. In these drafts, though, players typically compete in the league they were drafted in the following season.[31] This means players can be drafted to many junior leagues, but whatever league players decide to take part in, they must compete for the team that drafted them unless their rights are traded to another franchise. Drafts typically take place at different points toward the end of hockey seasons, so be sure to look into when your preferred league's draft occurs.

---

31   There are some exceptions to this though. Some leagues, like the USHL, have a "futures draft" in which younger players' rights to play in the league in which they have been drafted are reserved by certain franchises for years, not just the upcoming season.

TENDERS

Some players are asked to sign contracts called "tenders" before certain junior league drafts take place. Signing a tender reserves a player's rights and prevents any other team from doing so in the upcoming draft. However, programs only have a certain number of tenders to offer depending on the league, so teams generally are selective. It is important to note that in most leagues, although there are exceptions, whether a player is tendered or drafted does not mean they have made the team; rather, it indicates the program has reserved the player's rights, barring the player from being on any other team's roster in that league unless their rights are traded to another franchise. Being drafted or tendered is a great step toward making a team, but it is by no means a guaranteed spot in most leagues.

As a player, tendering to a team is beneficial because the player gets to choose where they would like to potentially play rather than being chosen by any team during the draft. The team, in return, gets to reserve rights for players they believe will make a big impact for their program. But again, in most leagues, tendering does not guarantee a spot on a roster—players still need to earn their spots and work to keep them throughout the year.

TRAVEL

Juniors entailed a lot more travel than I previously experienced in youth hockey. Not only are there a lot of long bus rides both pre- and post-game, but also the travel itself requires a high level of player professionalism. The travel can vary greatly by league, region, or team, but it is usually more extensive than players' youth programs. In Janesville, for example, our shortest trip was a three-hour drive, and our longest was a ten-hour flight to Alaska.

Learning how to travel and still perform at a high level is part of the junior experience. Although these trips can be great for team bonding, they can be a challenge to get used to as well. Responsibility for gear, clothes, and miscellaneous travel items; navigating differences between time zones; not letting travel disruptions affect performance on the ice; and managing physical exhaustion are all things that can take time to adjust to.

PRACTICES

Another aspect of being a true pro in juniors is navigating practices. In my experience, practices were a lot more intense, competitive, and focused than in my previous hockey endeavors. Every repetition in practice counts now. Players are competing day in and day out for ice time, lineup spots, and the chance to continue their hockey career past juniors. Adapting to this level of intensity can be challenging as well.

Additionally, practices can become repetitive over a long junior hockey season. Being able to bring your best, consistent effort for such an extended period of time can be the difference between players who move on and those who do not. This level of competence takes time to develop, and it's in juniors where players begin to do so.

AGENTS AND ADVISORS

As you've likely gathered by now, the world of junior ice hockey can be confusing to navigate. That's where hockey agents and advisors can be useful. They are not necessary for a player to move on to the next level, but some families and players find them very helpful. There are some key differences between hockey agents and advisors that are important to understand.

AGENTS

Agents work with players who are ready to make the jump to the professional ranks. They're typically not paid until players sign a contract, and the agent then receives a percentage of that contract. A very important thing to note is that players are not allowed to have agents and also be eligible to play in the NCAA. The NCAA wants to maintain a level playing field for young athletes; they do not want some young players receiving financial benefits others may not be able to receive. For players who want to play in the NCAA, since they cannot use an agent's services, they may want to work with an advisor.

ADVISORS

If players choose to hire an advisor, they are still eligible to compete for an NCAA program in the future. Differing from agents who are paid a percentage of a future contract, advisors are typically paid upfront by families of young hockey players. Advisors may help with the recruitment process for both colleges and juniors, and make sure that players are complying with NCAA regulations to maintain their amateur status. Additionally, they may provide information about different junior teams and leagues, as they usually have strong connections. They can help families and players ask their prospective teams the right questions, as well as help with the negotiation process during recruitment.

Some people in the hockey world are very skeptical when it comes to hockey advisors. While there are some great people who are advisors, there are also those who are more interested in financial gain than helping a player's career. As with all aspects of navigating their paths through hockey, it's important for players to research an advisor before working with them. Be sure to look at their website, learn about the clients they work with, and ask around in your community. Be cautious of advisors who promise a player a scholarship, or if a scenario feels too good to be true.

Here are some "Dos and Don'ts" from College Hockey Inc. regarding interactions with advisors:

- **Do not** accept gifts of any kind from an advisor, including money, meals, travel expenses, equipment, etc.

- **Do not** enter into an agreement—either signed or verbally—to have an advisor represent the player as an agent in the future.

- **Do not** ask the advisor to market your player's abilities to professional teams.

- **<u>Do</u>** plan to compensate the advisor for their services; failure to do so may be considered the player receiving a gift from the advisor, which would be an NCAA violation. This compensation shouldn't be extravagant—do not expect that one advisor is more valuable simply because they charge more. You don't always get what you pay for.

CHAPTER FOUR

LIFE AS A JUNIOR HOCKEY PLAYER

THE BILLET SYSTEM

Although some programs house players in apartment buildings or houses, many teams' players live with host families, known as "billets." To determine whether a billet family is a good fit, players typically fill out a housing questionnaire with their preferences including whether they'd like to live with another player, if they're allergic to any pets, if they have any dietary restrictions, or similar. The team's billet coordinator will then match players with housing situations that hopefully work well for everyone. Players usually receive their housing assignments within a few weeks prior to reporting for training camp.

There have been, and probably will continue to be, cases where billets do not have their heart in hosting junior hockey players. However, for the most part (and as was the case with all of my billet families), billets welcome players with open arms. They're truly the unsung heroes behind junior hockey franchises, and these programs could not operate without them.

Like any family, billets come in all different shapes and sizes: some families billet many players, others have kids of their own at home; some have high-profile jobs, some do not; some are billeting for the first time, while others have been doing it for twenty years. Additionally, some billets may expect certain things from their players—they may want them to help out around the house or pick up their kids from school. Some hope their players are integrated into their family, while others are happy to give their players space.

In retrospect, since there are so many different billet families out there, the best advice I can give to create an ideal situation for everyone involved is for all parties to have honest conversations from the beginning about what they are expecting. It's normal to feel nervous about living with a family that you've never met. But many players have incredible, positive, and long-lasting relationships with their billet families, who treat them like their own.

WHAT JUNIOR HOCKEY PLAYERS DO OFF THE ICE

Despite spending a lot more time on the ice, in the gym, or watching film than they're used to, junior hockey players are still often left with a lot of free time. What do they do with these breaks? This varies from player to player, but there are a lot of options for athletes to fill the hours: part-time jobs, taking college or high school courses, or volunteering in their communities.[32] And, of course, there are lots of videogames played and quality time spent with teammates outside the rink. It's through all that time spent together though that junior hockey teams become so close.

DROPPIN' THE MITTS

Players' lives off the ice in juniors can be a lot different than they are used to, and on the ice, they can likely expect some adjustment as well. In both youth and college hockey, fighting is not allowed. However, in the gap years between the two levels in juniors, the gloves can come off.

---

32   Players cannot be full-time students while playing junior hockey; this would trigger their "eligibility clock" to begin. At the NCAA Division I level, players have five calendar years to play four athletic seasons once they are enrolled as a full-time student.

Scrapping has been a part of the sport for a long time, and it's at least one reason that many fans watch games.[33] However, the culture surrounding fighting in hockey may be different than some may expect. Sometimes fights start because players are pissed off; sometimes it's to protect a teammate; sometimes it's to send a message to an opponent; but every now and then, a fight breaks out to change the momentum of a game—and sometimes, the events leading up to that momentum-changing tussle are bizarre to those who aren't familiar with fighting culture in hockey.

Players from opposing teams will sometimes talk to each other before a game, in warmups, or at a faceoff. Topics of discussion usually include some jokes, the game the night before, or having a mutual friend. But sometimes, even more interestingly, players may discuss starting a fight on purpose. If an agreement is reached, players will drop their gloves—or "mitts"—when the time is right and trade blows with each other, to fans' delight. After the scuffle, they may congratulate each other on a job well done as they skate to the penalty box listening to

---

33   Rodney J. Paul, "Variations in NHL Attendance: The Impact of Violence, Scoring, and Regional Rivalries." *The American Journal of Economics and Sociology* 62, no. 2 (2003): 345–64, https://doi.org/10.1111/1536-7150.00216.

the symphony of cheers from teammates and spectators alike.

When I was loaned up to Lincoln for those two weeks while I was still playing for the Jets, I had my first experience with fighting culture in hockey. I was stretching on the ice in warmups before the game when the opposing goalie skated up to me, congratulating me on the call-up. I thanked him, and he proceeded to ask me if we were "going tonight." Since fighting was non-existent in high school hockey, my reply was upbeat and naïve: "Yeah I got the start tonight!"

The opposing goalie laughed, shaking his mitts, the signal for asking for a fight. "No, are we *going* tonight?"

Realizing what was going on, and being so focused on playing well while I was called up, I quickly declined and skated away. Rookie mistake.

I thought that was the end of it, but then the game started. It was a rivalry game, and it got chippy quick. There were 29 penalties called between the two teams, tallying up to 144 penalty minutes on the evening. Toward the end of the game, a brawl broke out on my end of the ice. I stood in the net, enjoying the show, my arm perched up on the crossbar. However, I didn't see that at the other end of the rink, the opposing goalie was standing at the blue line, waiting for me to notice him and to meet at center ice for a rare sight—a goalie fight. I didn't know that's what was going on, but knowing who I was back then, I probably wouldn't have been bold enough to skate down there and take him on. If I have one regret from juniors, it's not getting in a fight. (Don't worry—my brother gives me grief for this one repeatedly).

As much as some fans enjoy watching players battle it out with their fists, some are calling for an end to fighting in hockey.[34] Some argue that having players fight at a young age can be harmful, especially if it's a sixteen-year-old going up against a twenty-year-old.

In 2011, long-time NHL fighter Derek Boogaard passed away by overdose, and some believe it was caused in part by the toll his fighting-heavy career took on his physical and mental health.[35] On that note, in the

---

34 Charles A. Popkin, "Ban Fighting in the NHL," *The Boston Globe*, November 24, 2022, https://www.bostonglobe.com/2022/11/24/opinion/ban-fighting-nhl/; John Branch, "Junior Leagues Ponder Banning Hockey Fights," "Rules to Be Stiffened," "'Our Ultimate Goal Is to Remove Fighting,' Hockey Canada Says," *National Post*, February 29, 2012.

35 Branch, "Derek Boogaard: A Boy Learns to Brawl," *The New York Times*, December 3, 2011, https://www.nytimes.com/2011/12/04/sports/hockey/derek-boogaard-a-boy-learns-to-brawl.html; Branch, "Derek Boogaard: A Brain 'Going Bad,'" *The New York Times*, December 5, 2011, https://www.nytimes.com/2011/12/06/sports/hockey/derek-boogaard-a-brain-going-bad.html.

documentary *Ice Guardians*, notorious NHL enforcers discuss the struggles and anxieties they faced in their own lives as a result of being on-ice fighters. The debate over whether fighting should be permitted in juniors continues today, but for now, it's part of the game, and players should be ready for it for the first time in their hockey careers when they make the jump to juniors.

HEY LOOK MA, I MADE IT!

As of April of 2020, my hometown has a population of 5,467.[36] Needless to say, it's a small town—it was rare to walk into a store in town and not see someone you knew, and for me, there wasn't a ton to do growing up besides playing hockey.

Also as of April of 2020, Janesville, Wisconsin, where I played my first year of juniors, has a population of 65,615.[37] Coming from my town of five thousand people, going to Janesville was the equivalent of heading off to the big city. People knew the Jets around town—there were advertisements for our games on the radio and we were a

---

36   U.S. Census Bureau, "QuickFacts: Chelsea city, Michigan," https://www.census.gov/quickfacts/fact/table/chelseacitymichigan/HSG445221.

37   U.S. Census Bureau, "QuickFacts: Janesville city, Wisconsin," https://www.census.gov/quickfacts/janesvillecitywisconsin.

highlight in the city parade. People would ask for my autograph after games, and my jersey would sell for hundreds of dollars at charity events. Moreover, there were more than just a handful of stoplights in the town. I thought I made it big time.

There was one moment at the annual NAHL showcase in Blaine, Minnesota that sums up the transition from playing high school hockey in Michigan to juniors. At this event, many college and professional scouts as well as advisors flood the rinks to watch the upcoming season's prospects. It is in this showcase that scouts and advisors often get their first glimpse of who they are interested in, and where final rosters are made for the NAHL.

My parents made the trip to the showcase in Minnesota to watch me play when I competed for the Jets. At one point, my mom was doing what thousands of hockey moms do at their children's tournaments: taking pictures of me so she could proudly post them on her Facebook. While she was snapping away, a man walked up next to her, pointing. "Is that your son out there?"

"Yeah, I'm out here to watch him play." Right then, she noticed his jacket. He was a scout for an NHL club. He smiled. "Yeah, I'm here to watch him play too."

As you can imagine, she just about fell over with excitement. The very next week, I landed on NHL central scouting—the list that tabs the top prospects for the upcoming NHL draft.[38] Thanks, Mom!

I had a lot of "Hey Look 'Ma, I Made It!" moments. Looking back, I laugh at how I thought I had made it to the big leagues. In juniors, players compete in much smaller towns compared to NHL franchises or colleges, they're being heavily recruited, and in a lot of places, there's huge fan support. Although it's definitely not anywhere close to making it to the NHL, athletes can expect a different overall experience in juniors than they had in their youth programs prior.

38   Mason Lyttle, "Schaedig, Novak Placed on NHL Central Scouting." October 4, 2016. https://www.janesvillejets.com/schaedig-novak-placed-on-nhl-central-scouting.

CHAPTER FIVE:

COMPETE, COMPETE, AND COMPETE SOME MORE

At any junior, college, or professional hockey game, there are twenty or so hardworking, talented players on the ice. However, there are also a handful of other hardworking, talented players who are equally on the team, but they're seated up in the stands, dressed in suit jackets and ties instead of their equipment. They didn't make the lineup that night. The very next night, one of those same players who was dressed to the nines might be on the ice while you cheer them on, and another player will take their previous place in the stands. These dapper individuals are called "healthy scratches," and being one while watching your teammates compete without you is a shock for many young players.

Junior hockey is competitive. Let me try that again—junior hockey is *extremely competitive*. To put into perspective just *how* competitive, let's first take a look at the chances of making it to NCAA Division I ice hockey, the highest level of amateur hockey in the US, and the goal for many young players. As of 2023, there are sixty-two

NCAA Division I ice hockey programs.[39] To merely get on one of these teams is an extremely difficult task. In 2018–19, only 4.8% of high school players managed to crack the rosters of one of these elite-level squads.[40] In contrast to the sixty-two Division I programs, the USHL has only sixteen teams. Needless to say, to play in one of the top junior leagues is a journey in and of itself. Mine started in my junior year of high school.

In my third year of high school, my coach recommended I go to a junior camp to get exposed to that level of play. My family and I drove to Springfield, Illinois, and I attended the tryout camps of the Springfield Junior Blues in the NAHL. After going to their pre-draft camp, I was lucky enough to be invited back for their main camp. To my surprise, I made the all-star game, cutting the tryout camp roster down to just four goalies. Soon after I received this news, I had a meeting with the head coach of the Junior Blues.

---

39   U.S. College Hockey Online, "Men's Division I PairWise Rankings." https://www.uscho.com/rankings/pairwise-rankings/d-i-men/.

40   National College Athletics Association, "Men's Ice Hockey: Probability of Competing beyond High School." NCAA.org, April 20, 2020. https://www.ncaa.org/sports/2015/3/6/men-s-ice-hockey-probability-of-competing-beyond-high-school.aspx.

He looked me over. "If I offered you a spot on this team, would you take it?"

Being a naïve seventeen-year-old who hadn't expected to make it to that point and wanting to compete for my high school my senior year, I told him I wasn't sure. He simply raised his eyebrows in a sign of his shock.

Needless to say, I did not end up making the Junior Blues roster that year. When I returned home, my goalie coach gave me one piece of advice: "If a junior hockey coach in one of the top leagues asks you if you will take a spot on his team, just say 'yes.'" Lesson learned.

As a senior in 2016, I was named the best goalie in Michigan high school hockey for the year. My team and I lost the state semi-finals in overtime, facing fifty-three shots on the night. I sulked into my seat for the bus ride home knowing this was my last time playing with my childhood friends. But then, reality sunk in: I hadn't gotten an offer from a single junior hockey team, let alone a college. *What am I going to do now?*

I took some time off from hockey after a long season, but not too long, because tryouts for junior teams were coming up fast. Most of my senior teammates had just played their last competitive hockey game, and the rest were either taking extended time off to rest or playing other sports in the spring. I was left with no one to shoot on me. This is a bit of an issue, being a goalie.

I knew I had to stay on the ice to be ready for junior tryouts. I worked out, focused on my edgework, and honed my hand-eye coordination off the ice. I would find shooters every now and then at sticks-and-pucks—open ice at local rinks—or a former teammate would make an occasional appearance when they could. For the most part, though, I skated by myself, readying my game and hoping a team would take a chance on me. Ironically, it was during this time that my skating ability developed immensely and became one of the strengths that propelled me through my junior career.

I began making my rounds on the junior hockey tryout circuit. After my high school season ended, I was invited to practice with the Springfield Junior Blues. A few practices later, the head coach told me he liked what he saw in my game but that they were still assessing their goalie situation. I was still without a team. So, my dad and I got in the car and drove thirteen hours to Wayne, New Jersey—I had another tryout to get to. The New Jersey Hitmen are typically one of the top contenders in the USPHL, and their head coach had seen me play at a

tournament in Minnesota. He's who invited me to
tryouts.

After making the road trip with my dad from Illinois to
New Jersey, I competed against the other goalies at that
year's camp. After a few days of goalie drills and
scrimmages, I got called into the head coach's office. The
good news was he was offering me a spot on the team; the
not-so-good news is there were two other goalies already
signed for that year. Moreover, the top league in the
USPHL was pay-to-play at the time. I would be paying
thousands of dollars to have a chance to beat out the other
two goalies, one of whom won goaltender of the year the
season prior. I had a choice to make: sign with the Hitmen
and outplay the other two goalies, or look for another
opportunity elsewhere.

Ultimately, despite the Hitmen's proven track record
of advancing players to the next level, I chose to take a
chance on myself in hopes of finding something better.
Still without having another place to play, I decided to not
sign with the Hitmen and set my sights on making a team
in the NAHL. My dad and I got back in the car and started
the trek back to Michigan. We had more tryouts to get to.

When I was trying to make a junior team, I received
many emails inviting me to participate in pre-draft

camps. After doing some research on the teams, I attended a few. Almost every weekend, I headed to rinks across southeast Michigan to try to convince a team I was good enough to make their roster. I got offered tenders from two teams in the NAHL: the Johnstown Tomahawks and the Janesville Jets. My eventual coach sent over the contract, and I signed with the Janesville Jets one morning before heading off to school for the day.

Although being tendered by the Jets was a good sign, I knew it was no guarantee. Another junior franchise offered me an additional path as a backup. The Metro Jets, who at that time competed in the NA3HL and are now a part of the USPHL, helped me throughout my junior hockey career. They knew I was looking to advance to the NAHL, but they decided to offer me a tender anyway, in case I didn't make Janesville's roster. Although I never ended up wearing a Metro Jets jersey, I am forever grateful for that program. They always prioritized my development, and they were one of the first junior teams who believed in me.

Although Johnstown is an amazing franchise, I ended up choosing to tender with Janesville because of their outstanding record of moving goaltenders on to the next level. Over 85% of the goalies who had played ten or more games for the Jets in the five years before I played moved on to play in the NCAA.[41] However, I wasn't the only one interested in playing for a program with so much success in advancing goalies.

When I got to main camp, I was one of forty-two goalies trying out that year for two open spots—and that was a luxury, as sometimes one or both goalies return from the previous year's team. The main camp started with two days of the large group of us battling it out in various goalie-specific drills in an effort to make it past the first round of cuts. After these two days, the goalie roster was shortened to twenty. The last two days of main camp included scrimmages between the ten teams of players also competing for a spot on the upcoming season's roster. Eventually, the coaching staff selected the rosters for the all-star game. Thankfully, I managed to make it to this point.

After the all-star game, each player was given a meeting with the coaching staff to discuss their performance and whether they would be invited back for training camp. My meeting was with the goalie coach. Filled with anxious energy, I walked into the room. My

41 Janesville Jets Goalie Statistics, https://www.janesvillejets.com/stats/player-stats/all-teams/271?playertype=goalie.

to-be coach gave me the news: I made the cut. I was coming back for the training camp and was one step closer to making the team. I beamed.

"Out of curiosity, what other goalies are coming back for training camp from this year's main camp?" I asked.

"You're the only one. We think we can find a better fit for a goalie on this year's team somewhere else." My to-be coach calmy responded.

I was stunned. Out of *forty-two* goalies trying out that year, they selected *one* to come back for preseason. Only one.

Like I said, juniors is *extremely competitive.*

After returning home to train for a few weeks, I packed up my car and drove back to Janesville for preseason. I, along with two other goalies at training camp, would compete over the next few weeks to earn the two available spots.

To this day—and I'm sure my former Jets teammates will agree with me on this one—training camp in Janesville was one of the most physically and mentally strenuous weeks I've ever experienced. It was filled with long and difficult off-ice workouts and skating sessions (I would call them practices, but we were lucky if we got to touch pucks at that point). After a week of pushing ourselves to bring the team together and show our dedication to being Jets, I finally got to see some shots a couple days before we played our first preseason game against the Bloomington Thunder, a former USHL franchise. After a close contest, we ended up winning—we knew we did *not* want to find out what next week's training would look like if we lost.

While we were busy fighting to make the Jets' roster, the players in the USHL were doing the same for their respective teams. After the USHL rosters were slimmed down, there were a lot of players still without a place to play for the year. That's when the trickle-down extravaganza begins.

Those players who were cut from the USHL franchises then try to make teams in other leagues, including the NAHL and including the Jets. Back in Janesville, after competing for a few weeks against the other players in training camp, players from the USHL were invited to join the team before the NAHL's roster deadline. Players who started the preseason in Janesville then trickled down to other teams in the NAHL or lower leagues, and the chaos ensued.

After the dust settled from the USHL players coming down to the NAHL, the stage was set to select the team in

Janesville. At this point in the tryout process, there were three goalies left, and only two were going to make the cut. As the roster deadline grew nearer, the tension rose.

I was getting ready for practice with my teammates just a few days before the roster deadline when my coach called me into his office. If you've seen the movie *Miracle*, then you know this isn't a good sign at that point in the season. As my coach headed back to his office, waiting for me, my teammates and I glanced at each other, all acknowledging the immensity of the moment.

The next five minutes were a blur. While it seemed like my mind went numb, I watched as my coach's mouth continued to form words I struggled to decipher. I did my best to focus—but this wasn't how it was supposed to go. I was poised and ready for my first junior season with the Jets, and now I was the first goalie called into my coach's office right before the trade deadline. His mild tone and his face full of apology provided little encouragement in the moment. As words continued to roll out, I mustered replies to his questions about my performance in training camp. I could feel his tone start to lower and readied myself to hear that I didn't make the cut. Then I heard a loud *slap*—a book, on his desk. Suddenly everything came back into focus.

The book was an equipment catalogue. "We're going to need you to pick out your sticks for the year." His grin was mischievous. Having been a part of the roster selection process as a junior hockey coach for nine years up until that point, he was always in for a good joke.

"Thank you, coach," I giddily replied. Unable to contain my excitement, I picked out my sticks and returned to my teammates having felt like I just dodged a bullet.

I had anticipated this moment for years. *Finally*, I was on an elite junior team.

I expected a huge sense of relief, but I didn't find one. It hit me: a spot on a junior hockey roster is never set. I knew that now. I was so focused on making it to that point in the selection process that I hadn't considered the reality of juniors. Even after I "made" the team, I could be cut from the squad or traded to another team at any given moment.

After many tryout camps, being cut from a lot of teams, being named the best goalie in Michigan high school hockey, signing tenders, beating out the forty-one other goalies at Janesville's main camp, a grueling training camp, and performing to the best of my ability in the preseason games, the competition never ends—a lesson that I had to learn, and one my coach in Janesville helped me see.

CHAPTER SIX

JUNIOR HOCKEY TRADITIONS

THE GOLDEN RULE

If you have never stepped foot in a hockey locker room, there is one rule you must know, the golden rule: *do not step on the logo*. In a lot of hockey locker rooms, the team's logo is placed on the ground in the middle of the room. As a sign of respect toward the team and the players who have contributed to the history of the franchise, players, coaches, and staff alike refrain from stepping on the emblem. Punishments for doing so vary by team. They can range from paying a small fine to doing some sort of strenuous physical activity, but the tradition is typically taken seriously among members of the club. So, if you ever find yourself walking around in a hockey locker room, avoid the logo at all costs.

COURT

As discussed in Chapter Four, athletes have a lot of free time in junior hockey. Because of this, players get creative with how they fill their hours. One of these ways is through the ritual known as "court." Junior hockey players, although sometimes treated like professionals, are still young adults. As parents reading this book may be able to relate to, that means they make a lot of mistakes. But, like all young people, they also do some pretty amazing things. That's where court comes in.

Although there are different ways court is carried out from team to team, the general idea is that the team implements a fines or rewards system for things deemed worthy. Court is typically held in the locker room once a week or so after the team is done training for the day. There are many ways to run court sessions, one being to go around the room one by one. Each player is given a turn to either fine a teammate or give away a credit for something someone did that week deserving of those convictions.

For example, if a player did not pick up pucks after practice when he was supposed to, that's a dollar fine. Didn't sweep the locker room? Dollar. Fell in warmups that week before the game? Dollar. Moved the nets after practice when it wasn't their responsibility? Credit. Helped a player out with their hockey laundry? Credit.

After all players have been given a turn to hand out their punishment or reward, then the court's designated treasurer sends out the week's list of credits and fines. Some players then owe the team a small amount of money, and a few will receive some. Once all credits and fines are tallied up, all money from court proceedings goes towards team bonding activities.

I should note that court can sometimes be a negative experience for some. When court isn't run properly, players sometimes impose hefty fines on others. Some may not find the ritual to be enjoyable. However, in my experience, court is a mostly positive tradition. On my teams, if a player could not afford to pay the fines they received, the treasurer would waive the debt and keep it anonymous. Generally, the fines were no more than ten dollars each week, and there was a limit on how much an individual could be fined.

The court ritual includes a lot of storytelling about what various teammates did on and off the ice in the last week, both good and bad. There are a lot of chirps—smack talk—thrown around, and a lot of laughs as well. Court is one of the places where teams bond the most, and it's home to some of my favorite memories in my hockey career.

BEER-A-MID

Between the University of Wisconsin-Madison Badgers, the Green Bay Packers, and the Janesville Jets, if there's one thing that I learned about Wisconsin in my time playing hockey there, it's that Wisconsinites love beer. The beer-a-mid is a perfect example of just how much.

At Jets games, when the team would go on a powerplay, the beer is discounted. Being so, Jets supporters *love* powerplays. As soon as a penalty is called, the fans rush to the concessions stand to get their cheap hoppy beverage. Needless to say, there are a lot of empty beer cans left over after the game ends. Sure, they could go straight to the recycling bin, but where's the fun in that? Instead, fans stack up the cans into pyramids on the glass, sometimes up to four feet high. After the Jets win a game, players will check the glass, knocking the beer-a-mid down to everyone's delight. I got to do this one time in my final home game with my closest friend on the team, and that memory is one I'll cherish forever.

SEWER

In juniors, players develop both on and off the ice, and the game known as "sewer" is no exception. The activity is sometimes played before players get to juniors and after players move on to higher levels of hockey, but it's in the long junior hockey season that players truly develop their sewer skills. It is indeed the game before the game.

In this pregame ritual, players gather in a circle. The goal is to be the last person standing. Pitted against each other, players proceed to kick a soccer ball in the air without letting it touch the ground. Players get two touches before they have to advance the ball to the next competitor, and they can use anything but their arms to keep the ball in the air. If a player is the last one to touch the ball before it hits the ground, they're out. Additionally, the first one out of the game is asked to perform a dance of their choosing in front of the other players.

If a player purposefully tries to get an opponent out by kicking the ball at them in a way that makes it difficult to keep in the air, this is called a "sewer." The game usually starts out with a lot of nice players, but once the number of players dwindles down, all bets are off. It's every person for themselves, and there's only one winner in the end.

JUICEBOY

If sewer is the game before the game, then Juiceboy is the game after practice. It occurs immediately following the practice before gameday. Players compete in a shootout, taking turns trying to best their goalies. If you score, you're safe; if you don't, you get back in line and wait for your next chance. Players continue trying to score until there are two left.

At that point, the entire team lines up on both sides of the goalie, smacking their sticks on the ice as a sort of drumroll for the final act. The last two players trade shots until one of them scores, and the last player standing scoreless is swarmed by his teammates in celebration of his losing effort.

The punishment for a loss varies. Some teams have the losing player wear an embarrassing jersey on the ice; some have him untie other players' skates; some have the player serve juice to all his teammates, making him the "Juiceboy." If you've ever wondered where hockey players develop those highlight reel shootout moves you see on television or social media, it's probably in Juiceboy.

SHNARPS

Junior hockey players travel a lot with their teams. While typically not quite traveling via yellow school bus, teams don't usually have the luxury of flying to competitions either. Being so, this results in long bus rides with a lot of time to kill. One way that players pass the time is by playing card games, and a game that's been popularized by both junior and professional hockey players is known as "Shnarps."

There are lots of rules in Shnarps and learning them, as well as mastering the art of the game, is a rite of passage for some junior hockey players.[42] Not every player has to or does learn to play Shnarps, but if you do, then you can officially say you've made it to juniors.

---

42   If you would like a more detailed explanation of Shnarps and to try the game out for yourself with more guidance, you can check out the app "Shnarps – Classic Card Game" on the Apple App Store.

SHOE CHECK AND BUS TAG

In juniors, while players are busy developing their game on the ice as well as their sewer game off the ice, they're also repeatedly given the distinct opportunity of working on their singing ability in public. There are two ways that players can be bestowed this honor: shoe check and bus tag.

Players eat a lot of meals as a team on the road. While bonds are being formed above the table, there is no room for friends underneath. In the game "shoe check," while players eat, teammates begin to plot against each other to make their friend have to sing in public.

To do so, a player must sneak under the table and place some substance like ketchup or salt on a teammate's shoe. After the message has been sent, players begin to clang their glasses in unison as if egging on the bride and groom at a wedding. That's the notorious sign to look down at your shoes to see if you've been "shoe checked." If so, you are asked to stand up on a chair and belt out a song in front of the entire restaurant. Players need to be stealthy about their approach to placing the substance on a teammate's shoe though. If a player notices one of their teammates trying to shoe check them and catches the offender, then *they're* the one who gets to work on developing their vocal cords.

Even if you escape the clanging glass roar of shoe check, you're still not free from singing duties just yet. After the team is finished with their meals, it's time to load back onto the bus—but it's not quite that simple. As players leave, a game of tag ensues, with the first player out of the restaurant being "it." Teammates tag each other as they flood to the bus in a mass of hockey players, all eager to avoid another round of singing. The last one to be tagged gets to sing in the front of the bus right where the coaches typically take their seats.

Whether it's via shoe check or bus tag, I've heard some of the worst renditions of sing-alongs in my time in juniors but also some of the best memories. Juniors is full of unique traditions, and it is those moments that make the junior hockey experience truly special.

CHAPTER SEVEN:

A GAME OF INCHES

The legendary NFL head coach Vince Lombardi was once quoted saying "Football is a game of inches, and inches make the champion."[43] The saying has since been adopted by many sports and professions alike, and ice hockey is no different. In a game so fast-paced, the saying is particularly applicable—one inch to either side of the post off of a shot can be the difference between a goal, a championship, or a career.

There's another saying, this one from Roman philosopher Seneca, stating "luck is what happens when preparation meets opportunity."[44] This saying also applies to ice hockey. I am proud of the work I put in to be able to play college hockey, but I also recognize that in my story, and most likely in many others, luck played a large role in my ability to play high-level juniors and NCAA Division I hockey. Juniors is so competitive, and there are so many

43   Vince Lombardi, *The Essential Vince Lombardi: Words & Wisdom to Motivate, Inspire, and Win* (New York: McGraw Hill, 2002), 77.

44   Jill Griffin, "Luck Is What Happens When Preparation Meets Opportunity," *Forbes*, April 9, 2019, https://www.forbes.com/sites/jillgriffin/2019/04/09/luck-is-what-happens-when-preparation-meets-opportunity/.

elite players out there that the truth is, it takes hard work, talent, and luck to move on to the next level.

Although there were a lot of bounces that went my way to be able to finally suit up for the Crimson after playing at a high level of junior ice hockey, there were four major moments that could have taken me on a very different path from getting a college commitment. Remember the story of how I got called up to the highest junior league in the US in Lincoln from Janesville, won all four games with my team, beat Lincoln's rivals, won Co-goaltender of the Week in the USHL, and a few months later committed to play for Harvard? Sounds pretty amazing, right? Well, that story almost went a little differently. Following Seneca's famous quote, success came because I was prepared for the opportunity I was given, but I also got lucky.

The process of me getting called up to Lincoln was a lucky break in and of itself. There are a lot of goalies playing in the NAHL every year, along with elite goalies in other leagues, and Lincoln calling my coach out of all of them was huge. Even so, actually getting to play when I got called up was an even further stretch. When I agreed to go to Lincoln, I had no idea if I was going to be able to play or not, and neither did the coaching staff. One of their goalies had gone off to play in an international tournament, but they still had another very talented goalie on the roster. He was injured, and the coaching staff wasn't sure if he was going to be able to play for those two weeks I was called up.

But it ended up that the injured goalie was unable to play. Had either of these two goalies been able to compete, I probably would have never gotten the opportunity to play in the USHL that year. I most likely would not have been drafted in the first round of the USHL draft the following year, or potentially ever ended up playing in that league. Further, I may never have intrigued one of my dream schools. My hockey career completely changed with one phone call. That was bounce number one.

The second break I received came during that same playing stint with the Lincoln Stars. The week that I was named Co-goaltender of the Week, which sparked scouts' attention again, I faced sixty shots and allowed three goals, adding up to a .950 save percentage. My fellow Co-goaltender of the Week had a .963 save percentage that week. But, there is more to the story than the numbers might portray.

During the time I was named Co-goaltender of the Week, there was a goal called off due to a kicking motion by one of my opponents. Had he let the puck bounce off his leg without kicking, or had the referees seen the call differently, that goal might have counted. I would have then had a .934 save percentage instead of a .950. While still a respectable goaltending statistic, that save percentage may not have earned me Co-goaltender of the Week honors given that the other goalie had a .963 save percentage that week. Since this media attention is partially what reignited scouts' attention, I may never have piqued the interest of the Harvard coaches. That was break number two.

My third major bounce came one week in late January my first year playing for the Janesville Jets. My team and I were facing off against the Austin Bruins, and my coach informed me that one of Harvard's coaches were coming to watch me play. I was to start that Friday, and whether I played Saturday depended on my performance on that Friday night game.

I went into the game on Friday night feeling anxious. Both academically and athletically, Harvard was one of my dream schools. My team and I came out of the night with a 4–1 win, and I ended up with a .955 save percentage on the evening. My coach pulled me outside after the game, and I got to meet one of Harvard's coaches. He told me he liked my play, and he would continue to track my progress. I walked onto the bus unable to contain my excitement. The next day, my coach in Janesville elected to start me again.

Saturday night's game was a different story. I let up three goals on thirteen shots which left me with a .769 save percentage. I got pulled from the game halfway through and waited for what felt like an eternity to see if the Harvard coach was there again. I checked my phone after the game and found out he had to go to another game and did not witness my abysmal performance. Although I'll never know, I can't imagine he would have considered me in the same light for an offer to play for his program after seeing that game. I was lucky he came to see me on Friday and not Saturday. That was break number three.

Break number four came with an unusual beginning. Toward the end of my first year of juniors, the morning before a game, I woke up with a slight pain in my stomach. I went to the team's morning stretch as usual, but the pain slowly intensified. I continued to follow my gameday routine, though, and took my pregame nap. I was abruptly awakened by the pain in my stomach now at a searing high. I slumped my way into the kitchen, barely able to stand up straight, only to be stopped by my billet mom.

She took one look at me and knew something was up. "What on earth is wrong? Are you OK?"

At this point in the season, my goalie partner and I were battling for the starting job before heading into playoffs. I wasn't about to miss a game because of whatever nuisance was going on in my stomach.

"I'm fine," I grunted.

"No, you are not!" she fired back. "There is no way you can play tonight."

I knew she was right, so I called my coach to break the news. I went to the game, sat around during warmups, and watched my team play. After, I went to the hospital. The doctor knew immediately what was wrong: I had appendicitis and needed to go into surgery right away. I let my family back home, my billet family, and my training staff all know what was going on. When I awoke following surgery, all three parties were waiting for me at the hospital.

I hadn't been home in a few months, so I asked my coach if he would let me go back to recover for a few weeks. He gave me permission, and my family and I drove home to Michigan. A few days later, I received a phone call. It was a coach from the ice hockey program at the

University of Michigan. He asked me if I wanted to come on a visit now that I was back in the state.

Going into juniors, my top three dream schools were Harvard University, the University of Michigan, and the University of Notre Dame. By the time I was back home I had already been in communication with Harvard for a while, so to get a call from a coach at another one of my dream schools—the one I grew up thirty minutes down the road from and where my entire family had been employed at some point—well, I was elated to say the least.

So, I went on a visit to Ann Arbor. In my meeting with the coach, he told me he had only seen me play on film, but they would be out to see me play a couple weekends from then, and we'd discuss the potential of an offer.

After having an amazing visit at Michigan, I got another phone call. This time, it was Harvard's coach. "Did we lose ya to Michigan?" he joked, his thick Boston accent coming through the phone.

"No, it was just a visit."

"Good because we want you, Derek."

A few days later, Harvard offered me a spot on the team. The rest is history.

Had I not gotten appendicitis, I might not have been able to visit Michigan. Without that visit, there may not have been any pressure on Harvard to make me an offer, and I may never have been able to put on a Crimson sweater.

I worked hard for many years to be able to earn an opportunity to play high-level junior and college hockey, but I also got a lot of breaks—four, at least—in the process. The reality for me and for many players is, because there are so many elite hockey players out there, it takes more than just hard work and skill to advance. Sometimes it takes a little luck, and I am forever grateful for the bounces I received in my time in juniors.

CHAPTER EIGHT

WHY I LOVED JUNIORS

HOCKEY WAS A FULL-TIME GIG

The biggest reason I loved junior hockey is that it was the first time I finally got to focus solely on playing at my best. Growing up, I always had school and other extracurricular activities to balance alongside hockey, which are undoubtedly important. But playing juniors gave me the opportunity to put all of my energy into what I loved doing—playing hockey. I got to push myself and see how good I could really become.

Juniors is a unique time when the only thing players are expected to focus on is hockey. For the most part, they don't have academics like they did during youth hockey. Players can devote all their energy into being the best hockey player they want to be, a rare opportunity they will not have unless they reach the professional ranks one day.

THE BOYS

Time spent in practice, a hard-fought win, a devastating loss, hanging out with the boys after practice, or playing cards on taxing bus trips—these moments are when I became so close with my teammates. These bonds have lasted over many years, and I owe all of them to my junior hockey experience.

The season is a long one—it can become a grind at times. My teammates helped keep me motivated throughout the long year, and we pushed each other to get better every day. Without them, I would not have become the hockey player I was in my playing career. When it felt like I didn't have anything left in the tank, my teammates were by my side to help me through.

One of the coolest aspects of having these lifelong bonds is getting to see my former teammates' successes. I wanted to be the best I could be in my career, but I also cared deeply about their futures. If there was a way that we could all thrive and accomplish our dreams, that's what I wanted. To this day, every time I see one of them on TV in the NHL, I crack a smile knowing the boys finally made it.

THE FANS

Another reason juniors was such a special experience was the amazing fans in the towns I played in. In these smaller communities, residents love their hometown junior hockey team. As a young adult, getting to play in front of large crowds who cared enough about our team to want my autograph never ceased being amazing. I realized that the game of ice hockey is unique in its ability to bring people together. Putting on a show for these diehard fanbases every time I got to strap on the pads was something I didn't take for granted, and it is something I'll never forget.

WORLDWIDE FRIENDS

In my time as a junior hockey player, I played with teammates from Canada, Finland, Czechia, Sweden, Slovakia, and all over the United States. As many hockey families know, the hockey community is tight-knit and strong. Thanks to juniors, my own hockey community has expanded across the globe. I've gained so many new perspectives from my teammates and learned so much about where they come from. I didn't have much experience with folks from different backgrounds before

I got to juniors, but I came out with a new outlook on both hockey and life.

A LOT OF GROWING UP

Coming from a small town in Michigan, I did not know a lot about how the world works and how I fit into it before I went to juniors. This is the case for a lot of junior hockey players as it is the first time most of them have been away from home for an extended period. It is through juniors that I learned that I had a lot of growing up to do and learned about life. The game of hockey has taught me so much both on and off the ice, and it is through experiencing new aspects of life in juniors that I grew up the most in my playing career.

CHAPTER NINE:

...AND WHY I SOMETIMES DIDN'T

THE ADJUSTMENT TO LIVING AWAY FROM HOME

Just like when high school students go to college, a lot of junior hockey players move away from home for the first time in their lives when heading off to play juniors. This was an exciting experience for me, but it also came with a lot of challenges. Learning to be fully responsible for myself, living in a new home with a new second family, having an entirely new team, and playing at a much more competitive level of hockey all took time to adjust to. Sometimes I got frustrated with this process; I got homesick at times, and others I became tired of everything being new and difficult. I learned a lot about life in my first year through living away from home, but it wasn't always easy.

THE REALITY OF RECRUITMENT

Another new experience in the life of a young hockey player is being recruited by professional scouts, college coaches, junior programs, and/or advisors. When I was young, I imagined that magical day when I'd finally get to commit to play hockey for a Division I program. I pictured myself at a table among my loved ones with a few hats in front of me, each bearing a logo of one of the programs I had narrowed my selection down to. I'd choose one, sign the National Letter of Intent, and snap a few pictures.

But that's not how it went when it actually happened—I committed in a Walmart parking lot by myself because my billet family's house did not have the best cell reception.

Recruiting for professional hockey, colleges, juniors, and/or advisors to represent young players is filled with intense negotiations, quick deadlines to make important decisions, many phone calls and emails, and a lot of big, life-altering choices. Navigating this process can be tough, and the reality of being recruited can be different than many young players' expectations. Returning all the calls after practice while still striving to play well, trying to make one of the biggest decisions in my life for both my academic and athletic careers, and learning how to handle tough conversations were all aspects of the process I was unprepared for. Going through that process was trying for me and proves to be challenging for many other young players as well.

BEING A TRUE PRO... SORT OF

In juniors, players are treated as professional ice hockey players to some extent, even though they're not at that level quite yet. They can be cut and traded, and they're regarded as adults. They have those tough conversations with coaches, teammates, parents, and scouts alike. This approach, being seen as an independent, mature individual, helped me grow up quickly, but it was a hard transition.

FUNDING

Although junior teams do not typically fly across the country for a game the following day, as we know, junior teams do still extensively travel. But they do not have the funding NHL franchises do, making it hard for players to compete at the highest level.

For example: my first year of juniors, our glove dryer was a hole-covered PVC pipe attached to a hair dryer. Additionally, for the first part of the year, we had to travel forty-five minutes away to get our skates sharpened. One trip that we made to Alaska to play for a week, a few times we had to eat our meals out of the local convenience store. These things may seem minor, but when the difference between making that save and getting that scholarship comes down to the edge on your skate that day or how much energy you have left at the end of the game, the details matter.

Junior teams do the best they can with the funds they have, but without the same level of play and hockey market available to them, they just don't have the same kind of resources as bigger programs. This gap can be frustrating, and the difficulty varies from league to league, team to team, and player to player, but it is also something to expect and prepare for nonetheless.

IT'S A LONG SEASON

One of the first things I realized about juniors in comparison to my high school season is the length of the schedule: long. There are stark differences between NHL, NCAA, juniors, and high school schedules:[45]

- NHL: 82 regular season games over 6 months
- NCAA Division I: 34 regular season games over 6 months
- High school (Michigan): 25 regular season games over roughly 3 months
- USHL: 62 regular season games over 7 months

Needless to say, the junior hockey season is more like a pro schedule than a college or youth program. It's lengthy, and there's no doubt it's a grind.

Since teams typically practice and work out most days they're not playing games, the player's challenge then becomes maintaining a healthy body throughout the

---

45   These numbers are based on the 2022–23 seasons in each league. Tom Gulitti, "NHL Releases 2022–23 Regular-Season Schedule;" U.S. College Hockey Online, "About Division I Men's NCAA Hockey;" Michigan High School Athletic Association, "MHSAA Ice Hockey;" and United States Hockey League, "USHL Announces 2022–23 Schedule."

season. If a player develops a nagging injury, it becomes difficult to allow their body to heal. Because the leagues are so competitive, if they step out of the lineup for too long, they risk losing their starting spot. Players sometimes "tough it out" until the season is over, and those injuries can then finally resolve in the off-season. During the grueling season though, the toll on a player's body can be demanding.

Additionally, being able to perform at such a high-level night after night can be an adjustment. No matter how much a player loves the game—and most at this level do—practices can be trying or even repetitive. There will most likely be days players don't want to go to the rink. Even on those days, though, players must perform to stay in the lineup. And that's where the pressure of a long season builds.

PRESSURE

I loved pressure. Growing up I always thought that if I was going to train as hard as I could, eat the best way I knew how, and compete with everything I had, then I wanted to be in those moments where the game all came down to me. I loved the spotlight, so stepping in the net was the ideal position. But it's not just goalies who have to manage pressure—every hockey player faces pressure, and sometimes it can be crushing.

After such a long season, that very same pressure I loved so much growing up became difficult to manage. I felt like when I stepped onto that ice every day, what was most at stake was not just my playing time or my future but also, my way of life was on the line. If I didn't perform up to the coach's standards, I was at risk of being cut or traded and leaving my teammates, friends, and second family in my billets behind. Leaning how to handle that kind of stress takes time, but ultimately it was in doing so that I became prepared for many pressure-filled situations later in life.

GETTING TRADED

Before heading off to juniors, I felt like an excited kid on Christmas Eve. For months, I couldn't wait to work with the incredible players, chase my dreams, and be treated like a professional. I even went as far as thinking it wouldn't be *that* bad to be traded like those NHL stars I idolized. Be careful what you wish for, I guess.

In my first year playing for the Jets, I did not perform up to my own standards or my coaches. Coming into the season as a tendered goalie and playing in almost every game in the first quarter of the season, I ended the year as a backup, only playing once every couple of weeks, and I finished with a less-than-ideal .902 save percentage.

The USHL draft takes place toward the end of the season. Following my sub-stellar season, I didn't have high hopes. I remember asking my goalie coach if he thought I would get taken. He said he'd talked to a few teams, but he thought I might go in the fifth or sixth round because of those two weeks I played for Lincoln. When the draft came around, I was cooking breakfast at my billet house, keeping an eye on the results on my phone. Picks started to tick by. It was still the first round, so I wasn't watching the names that closely. But then, the fourteenth overall pick came in. The Chicago Steel had drafted me in the first round. I was so stunned I almost dropped the pancakes I was making that morning. Somehow, I had gotten a second chance.

A bit later in the season, my team and I had just lost out in the NAHL playoffs in the semi-finals. I sat in the locker room stall, having not played the entire postseason, tears rushing down my face. I knew my first junior season was finished, that I would never play on the same team with most of those guys ever again, and the reality that I did not live up to my performance expectations for the year sunk in. My coach came into the room and tried to offer words of encouragement to the team. My teammates and I got up and began our round of goodbye hugs, knowing we would most likely never all be in the same locker room together again. Afterwards, my coach called me outside.

He told me the Steel were in the playoffs—they were in the finals. They had run into some lineup difficulties, and they might need another goalie in the championship games. I couldn't believe it. I stood outside the locker room overwhelmed with a mix of emotions. I was relieved my stint of sitting the bench had come to a close, I was sad to leave my teammates, and now I was excited at the opportunity to play again.

As my teammates enjoyed some of their last moments as a team that night and grieved the loss, I sat on pins and needles wondering if I was about to step in for my new franchise. I waited all night for the call. It never came.

The next day, the Steel's general manager let me know they figured out their goaltending situation, and they wouldn't need me to come.

A week later when my tenure was finished with the Jets, I headed home to Michigan and stopped in to speak with the Steel coaching staff on my way. They ended up winning the league championship. Even though I hadn't been called up, they were excited about me; they thought I would be the top goalie and play around forty games the following year. I was thrilled. I had somehow been drafted in the first round in the highest league in the US to the best team in the league after a subpar season—I felt like I had hit the jackpot.

But then, because of the Steel's immense success as a franchise that year, the entire coaching staff took job offers in college and professional programs soon after I met with them. I knew what that meant. I was going to have to prove myself all over again to the new staff if I wanted a spot on the team. I trained hard all off-season, went to two of Chicago's tryout camps as well as their preseason camp, and I played well, but not incredible either. Days before the start of the regular season while I was getting ready for practice, my coach called me into the office. I sat there in full Chicago Steel attire, feeling similar to when my coach in Janesville called me into his office in preseason, but not *quite* the same. Somehow, this time felt different.

My coach in Chicago kept it simple: "Derek, you've been traded to Lincoln. I like your style, but that's the decision that was made. Best of luck to you."

I was shattered. So embarrassed. *How could this team's first round pick get traded?* My head spun. *Am I not good enough? Why don't they like me? What's my new team going to be like? Will I even play?*

I went home, packed up my belongings, and waited until my billet family returned home from work and school to say goodbye. As I turned out of that neighborhood in Illinois, I let it all out. I pulled over, and for a long time, tears came rushing down my face. I let out all of the pressure and embarrassment and anger I had in me. I yelled. I couldn't hold it in any longer. After I felt like I had released as much of what I was feeling as I could, I started my car and began the journey to my new home in Lincoln.

I ended up playing for Lincoln the rest of the season as a backup for the Stars. I competed in eighteen games— much fewer than the forty or so I was anticipating as a starter in Chicago. That shot to the ego was one of the hardest times in my life. After all, I was going into college the following year. *What is my Harvard coach going to think of a backup who barely played in juniors?*

Getting cut, traded, moved down leagues, or not playing is all very difficult to manage, especially for players who are used to being the stars of their team. This can be a part of juniors for many players, and it's important to react as well as possible if it happens. I wish I had accepted the role I was given earlier on in my career as a backup goaltender, but I learned a lot about myself in the process of doing so.

SOME GET BOUNCES, SOME DON'T

As I wrote earlier, players need to work hard and have talent to turn professional or get that scholarship. Usually, though, players do need to get a few bounces to get to the next level as well. Some players don't get them. For some, juniors isn't the best experience, and it ends up being where their hockey career comes to a close. Players can lose their love of the game, become burnt out, or get into bad situations.

I know so many talented and hard-working players who, for whatever reason, never made it to their ultimate goal. Junior hockey can be cruel at times and seeing this happen to my friends and teammates was hard. It added an element of fear too. *That guy is just as good as me, but he didn't move on*, I'd think. *Could that happen to me?*

I may never know why some of us get the bounces and some do not. I learned a tough lesson, a harsh reality: sometimes life isn't fair. This realization and seeing it play out in such a drastic way in juniors was difficult for me and can be for many others.

IDENTITY ISSUES

Like many athletes that make it to the junior ranks, I had been playing hockey for almost my entire life. It was all I knew—it made up who I was. I spent most of my days training, and when I wasn't, I was thinking about hockey. I removed anything in my life that could take me away from being the best goaltender I could. Hockey was everything. It was all that mattered to me.

Although everyone is different, many young junior hockey players have stories of sacrifices made for the game they love. To excel at a high level of a sport, it takes this level of commitment to become elite. Getting to play juniors was a dream of mine; all I ever wanted to do was play hockey and work on my craft, and I finally got to do so all year long. In the beginning of my junior career, I could not have been more excited.

This way of life worked well for me—until it didn't. When I was playing well, things were great: my team was winning games, my coaches were happy, and it felt like all my sacrifices were paying off. But everything revolved around hockey, including my self-worth.

Whenever I wasn't performing up to my standards, my world seemed to come crashing down. Besides the tension in the locker room that comes with a five-game losing streak, I felt like I wasn't good enough as a person. I couldn't separate Derek the goalie from Derek the human being. Hockey was all I knew, all I did, and all I thought about. I saw the same twenty or so players every day and focused intensely on the game from nine a.m. until two in the afternoon. Hockey was who I *was*. After all, what else was there, right? I was eighteen, and it was the lens through which I viewed the world—it was how I learned about the world, and it was all that that *mattered* to me in the world. If I wasn't playing well, I lost my sense of self-worth. I lost my identity.

Many hockey players, especially in juniors, struggle with their identity being tied up in the game alone. Sometimes they don't have friends outside of hockey, and some don't go to school or have a job. All they have is the game. It can become hard to separate life and hockey, or hockey and being human, for junior players especially.

I still struggle with how to approach this topic. We know players have to give their all to become elite and pursue their dreams, but this approach can be unhealthy on its own. I encourage players to chase those dreams, but while recognizing this vital life lesson—that balance in all areas of life is necessary not only to perform well but also to maintain a players' mental wellbeing. Hockey is a part of who these amazing athletes are, but it does not, and should not, define them.

THE CULTURE

I love ice hockey. It has taken me a long time to be able to say that sentence again and really mean it. I had to remind myself that I love the intensity of the game, its fast-paced nature, the close bonds I formed, and the feelings— pitching a shutout, the adrenaline rush before games, and gliding around a frozen pond on a cold Michigan night. I love the lingo, the post-goal celebrations, the traditions, the amazing people I have met over twenty years, and the life lessons it taught me.

I recognize everything the game has given me. Hell, I wouldn't even be able to write this book, let alone get to attend an institution like Harvard, without it. I can honestly say I still love hockey and recognize how beautiful it can be. It's had an indelible impact on my life, it guided me growing up, and it shaped the person I am today.

Yet, I still have a complicated relationship with the game, and that's due in part to the culture surrounding junior hockey. It can be taxing. Hockey is peculiar; it's violent, expensive, gear-heavy, grueling, and it has its own language—if "apple," "lettuce," or "grocery stick" mean no more to you than items at a supermarket, you need some hockey vocabulary lessons. Indeed, hockey has its own unique culture. While there are a lot of incredible aspects, there are negative ones, as well.

From what I've heard from generations prior, the issues I describe in this section have dramatically improved, but they're not altogether gone. As a community, we still have a long way to go regarding sexism, homophobia, and racism, among other issues still very prevalent in the sport we all love.

Ragging on teammates and trying to get in opponents' heads with one-liner chirps is a part of the game. It always has been, and I hope it always will be. Not only can chirps be quite comical, but they can also be used as strategic tools. Chirping opponents to throw them off their game is a legitimate approach in hockey, and some players are phenomenal at it.

There's room for chirping in the game, but sometimes I think its culture can be harmful. I'm a firm believer that words matter—they can hurt. They impact others. And personally, I find a lot of humor in teammates chirping each other's gear, when they fall during warmups, or their ability to play the NHL video game ("chel" in hockey jargon). But everyone has their idea of what lines can and cannot be crossed; what is a joke to some might not be funny to others. It can be difficult to determine where a person's boundaries are, but it is important to do so. Like I said, words can hurt. In a world that's becoming more and more careful with word choice and statements, chirping can be tricky to implement.

While I see the value in this culture and hope is never leaves the game completely, there are issues. When chirping goes from light-hearted jokes to sexist, homophobic, or racist slurs, even within the privacy of a locker room, that's an issue. Hearing these insults and pejoratives, like referring to women as "puck sluts," started to become more prevalent for me once I made the jump to junior hockey. Even toward the end of my career when people were being more frequently held accountable for this kind of behavior, these words were still embedded in some players' vocabularies. Very rarely are they hurled at opposing teams or the general public. Yet behind closed doors, they surface. These words and phrases and others like them do indeed matter; they come from harmful and hateful origins, and they can damage others.

When players joined a new team during my juniors career, one of the first things the new additions would do was give a formal introduction. Players stood up one by one in front of the team and listed off information about themselves. Most of it was pretty standard: name, position, hometown, and previous teams. But it also typically included the number of girls a player has had sex with, commonly referred to as "kills."

This tradition, and the attitude surrounding sex that comes with it, fosters a deeply harmful view of athletes' sexual partners, particularly women. Players are sometimes respected for having as many partners as possible, and some coaches even encourage and favor this hookup culture over dating for fear players will "get distracted" from their playing career if they have a committed relationship.

Sometimes, this culture goes further than words, carrying harsh consequences. In 2018, a young woman accused eight junior hockey players in the CHL of sexually assaulting her.[46] She was awarded $3.5 million in the settlement deal reached, and the scandal rocked the hockey world. As of 2022, it has been reported that since 1989, Hockey Canada has paid $8.9 million dollars to twenty-one individuals to settle sexual assault accusations.

Additionally, in my twenty years of playing hockey, I have played with a lot of different athletes, but I've never been on a team with an open member of the LGBTQIA+ community. There could be a number of reasons why this community is not as prevalent or openly out in junior hockey, but I believe one is the culture in junior hockey— at least sometimes in some spaces—still allowing homophobic behavior. The word "gay" is routinely used negatively. Something considered "lame" or not up to par is dubbed as "gay" by some players. That language sets the tone, providing free rein for anti-LGBTQIA+ sentiments, like intentionally harmful words like "faggot" being thrown around the locker room. There is an overall "otherness" of how players in general view these

---

46   Ashley Burke, "Crisis on Ice: What You Need to Know about the Hockey Canada Scandal," CBC, July 29, 2022, https://www.cbc.ca/news/politics/hockey-canada-sexual-assault-crisis-parliamentary-committee-1.6535248.

communities; in the sport's hyper-heterosexual culture, being a member of that community is seen as unusual.

Again, this often doesn't stop with language. When I played juniors, there was tradition known as "gay watch." If a player was deemed as acting "too gay," he was threatened with having to wear a swimsuit in the shower to supposedly protect him from getting an erection in front of his naked teammates. It's threats like these, as well as the vocabulary, the junior hockey community uses that make juniors an unwelcoming and unsafe place for athletes in the LGBTQIA+ community.

It's important to state that progress has been made in this area. In 2021, Luke Prokop made history by becoming the first player under contract to openly identify as gay in the NHL's 105-year history.[47] His announcement was met with support from his franchise, the Nashville Predators, along with NHL commissioner Gary Bettman, his teammates, and fans alike. However, anti-LGBTQIA+ notions are still prevalent. No matter an individual's opinion on members of these communities, the negative language used and traditions upheld among teammates

---

47 Amalie Benjamin, "Predators Prospect Prokop Comes out as Gay, Makes NHL History," NHL.com, July 19, 2021, https://www.nhl.com/news/nashville-prospect-luke-prokop-comes-out-as-gay/c-325686490.

affect these athletes' wellbeing. Not only do words matter, but so do actions, and it's imperative we continue to strive for progress.

In my experience, similar to the LGBTQIA+ community, the BIPOC community is also underrepresented in hockey. In 2020, only 5.7% of players on NHL rosters identified as BIPOC, compared to 83.1% in the NBA, 70.1% in the NFL, and 39.8% in the MLB.[48] I saw these statistics play out in my career. I have played with just two Black ice hockey players in the twenty years I've played hockey, and only one during my time in juniors. Racism and racist behavior still exist in both hockey players and fans alike. Whether it's a player throwing the N-word around in the locker room or a fan telling my Black teammate that "he should go back home and eat some fried chicken," racism remains at play. These words make the game an unwelcoming, potentially dangerous place for those in the BIPOC community, and they discourage those who want to put on the pads.

Juniors is a lot of players' first time on their own, and they are left alone to learn about early adulthood, including words they use and the way they treat others.

---

48   Benjamin, "Predators Prospect Prokop Comes out as Gay, Makes NHL History."

The younger players typically look up to their older teammates, who may be twenty or even twenty-one years old but are also still figuring out for themselves how they fit into the world, and often, trying to show they know what that looks like. The veterans teach the rookies, but the vets are still young themselves, and they make lots of mistakes. And the cycle repeats: harmful words and traditions get passed on, people get hurt or outcast from the game, and the negative culture festers.

Sexism, homophobia, and racism, among other issues, are still prevalent in junior ice hockey today. By no means is it everyone in the hockey community—after all, some of the best people I've ever met came from juniors. But it remains true that these issues are still very much alive.

At this point, it's important for me to mention that I am not exempt from having been part of the junior hockey culture. Although I took pride in not adding to the harmful elements as best I could, I was still a part of the problem for a long time. I have made mistakes, said and done things I regret, and I stood by too often; I did not do enough to change the culture until now, later in adulthood. But I wrote this chapter because I want my future kids to play hockey one day if they so choose, and I want one of their stops along their journey to be juniors. I want them to experience all the amazing aspects it has to offer, all the things I so enjoyed—getting to chase their dreams at such a young age, forming lifelong bonds with teammates, playing in front of many fans, making friends around the world, and growing up in this unique way. I hope that the culture continues to change for the better. I hope my future kids can play one day, be comfortable, and feel at home regardless of their race, sexual orientation, or any other identity they may have.

Both USA Hockey and Hockey Canada have protocols and organizations in place to continue to address the wellbeing of players.[49] Yet, I believe culture is created from within by the members of the community. To change the culture, players, coaches, families, and the rest of the junior hockey community need to take a stand and implement those imperative changes person by person.

The words we as a hockey community choose, along with the actions we take, affect others' wellbeing, the game we love, and who gets to play our amazing sport. Alluding to the NHL Diversity Task Force's "Hockey is For Everyone" campaign, Evan F. Moore said it best in the

---

49   Hockey Canada, "Hockey Canada Development Programs and Resources," https://www.hockeycanada.ca/en-ca/hockey-programs; USA Hockey, "USA Hockey Safe Sport Program," https://www.usahockey.com/safesportprogram.

book he coauthored with Jashvina Shah, *Game Misconduct: Hockey's Toxic Culture and How to Fix It*: "Hockey isn't for everyone until everyone shows up."

TEN LESSONS I LEARNED FROM JUNIORS

Juniors was home to some of the best and most challenging times of my life. I was both a starting goalie and a backup at times, and I had a lot of learning to do about both hockey and life. I had a lot of ups and downs, but I'm very grateful for everything juniors taught me. With that said, here are ten lessons that I learned from my time playing juniors.

1. HOW TO LIVE AWAY FROM HOME

Like most players, juniors was my first experience living away from home. I learned how to cook, do laundry, manage my time well, and be resourceful in the unique environment. In many cases, players' programs are far from home, and it's not uncommon to experience homesickness. Adjusting to living in a new place for the first time while being responsible for myself was one of the key lessons that juniors taught me.

2. HOW TO WORK HARD

My dad was a potato farmer for the first thirty-one years of his life. Although he took many lessons with him, the most prominent value he passed on to me is the importance of a strong work ethic. He continues to this day to make sure I remember that there is no substitute for hard work. He instilled that strong work ethic in me while I was growing up, but juniors was a whole other level. For the first time in my career, I was surrounded by other individuals who worked at perfecting their hockey craft every single day. Many of them had not just good but unbelievable work ethics, and them working so hard forced me to push even harder. Moreover, many of my teammates and opponents were more talented than I was—I had to work that much harder if I wanted to stay at that level. My time in juniors opened my eyes to the world of competitive athletics and showed me how important working hard is in hockey and in life, just like my dad taught me.

3. HOW TO LIVE A BALANCED LIFE

My dad was an expert in working hard, but he was not an expert in living a balanced life. How could he have been?

For any farmers reading, you know there isn't a lot of time for finding a healthy work-life balance. So I had to learn it on my own, the hard way—many times.

I gave everything I had to become the best hockey goalie I could be in my junior career. I mean *everything*. I ate as healthily as I could; I would allow myself only one "cheat meal" every month or so. Growing up, I frequently skipped Friday night high school football games because I played in an off-season league with early Saturday morning competitions. I did not drink alcohol or do drugs. I never skipped a rep in a workout or in practice. When I went home I watched film, stretched, or watched the Detroit Red Wings on TV. I ate, slept, and breathed hockey. For me, being that motivated helped get me to the level that I reached, but it wasn't sustainable. Eventually, I burned out.

I want to be careful to note here that loving the game of ice hockey and being motivated to get better is not merely a positive thing—it is absolutely necessary to become an elite player. But there is a fine line between being motivated and having an obsession with the game that can become too much for a player to manage both mentally and physically. I had to learn to give my all and chase my dreams while also taking time to enjoy things outside of hockey. If all a player has is the game, it can add unnecessary pressure in an already pressure-intensive sport. If players learn to manage a healthy work-life balance while working hard and competing, they'll be better players for it; they'll be happier on and off the ice, and when it comes time to work on their game, they'll be even more motivated and efficient than if all they did was eat, sleep, and breathe hockey.

Playing in a season as long, intense, and stressful as in juniors, I had to learn how to live a balanced life. The truth is, as much as I wanted to and felt I had to always be obsessing over hockey or I would be letting myself down, no one can work on hockey—or any sport—all day, every day. Even most NHL players, who are the best in the world at what they do, make time to do things they enjoy or to relax with family and friends. Having this healthy work-life balance was something I had to learn, and juniors taught me how.

4. HOW TO HANDLE ADVERSITY

Some of the hardest workers I know never got that NCAA scholarship they deserved or never made it to The League, while others who were more talented but lazier did. Sometimes, as I've discussed, life just is not fair.

In juniors, I had my fair share of goals I'd like back, below .900 save percentage performances, getting pulled from games, getting traded, and getting cut from teams. I applied that work ethic my dad fostered in me as best I could, but sometimes a puck hit off my teammate's skate or took a weird bounce and still went in. Things that were outside of my control affected the results I saw, and for the first time in my life, those had real consequences in my life both on and off the ice. I wasn't given the benefit of the doubt, given a long leash, or a guarantee that I'd play in the next game. The message in juniors was sometimes brutal but simple: produce good results, play again; don't produce good results, don't play again—no matter what.

I had to learn how to face daunting adversity for the first time as a player, and I've carried that with me. Before juniors, I had poor performances, let up soft goals, and lost big games, but never had I sat for weeks without playing, gotten traded, or been forced into a backup role. No matter who a player is, the odds are high they will face some serious adversity in juniors. Learning how to manage this very real adversity is key not just for success in players' hockey careers but in life after hockey as well.

5. HOW TO PLAY A ROLE

Due to my subpar performance as the starter in the first twelve of fifteen games of the regular season in Janesville, I was starting to lose my line-up spot. By season's end, I was the clear backup. I didn't play a single one of the nine games in playoffs.

Then I was drafted in the USHL. I thought it was my second chance—that I'd get to be a starter again. But then I got traded to Lincoln and only played in those eighteen games. I got a shutout in my last game of the regular season, and I remember thinking it felt just like Janesville. *You probably aren't going to play in playoffs, so that was a good way to end your junior career.* But my goalie partner struggled to find his rhythm, and I ended up playing in six of the eight playoff games for the Stars.

I played every role on the team a goalie can have in my junior career. At different points I was a clear starter, or I battled for the starting job, or I was a clear backup, or I was injured. This was all new to me—in my last three years of high school, I had started almost every game. I had to learn to accept the role I was given. It took time to embrace it, but once I did, my game improved drastically. I wasn't playing angry or putting as much pressure on myself. More importantly, I was a much better teammate once I did so.

In their youth programs, many juniors players were the stars of the team. But in these high-level leagues, *every* kid was the star of their youth programs. Not everyone can play that role again. While players should be competitive and shoot for that starting role, it's important to recognize that not everyone can have it and to embrace the opportunity a player is given, even if it is not what they envisioned before coming into juniors.

6. HOW TO MANAGE THE MENTAL SIDE OF THE GAME

In my first year of high school hockey, I didn't get to start a single game. The following year, I was the only goalie, and therefore started every game. The first game I finally got to start in, I got rattled and let up *eleven* goals. Needless to say, I had to learn how to manage the mental side of the game both on and off the ice.

As mentioned, juniors was filled with a lot more pressure than my previous teams, and I had a lot of worries. *Am I going to be cut or traded? When will I get to play again? What does the coach think of me? That last goal sucked. How am I going to bounce back?* I saw two options: either learn how to manage this new pressure and remain at a high level, or let it overwhelm me and lose out on my dream of playing college hockey. It was challenging, but over time I got there, with a lot of hard work. I still use that skill in my daily life.

Off the ice, I was struggling mentally. Being a goalie can be isolating and lonely. We're heroes when we steal the game, but not so much when we let in that soft overtime goal to lose the championship. We play a specialized, unique role that not many people are experts at. Sometimes goalies can be outcasts.

The reality of goaltending, along with the different roles I was placed in during juniors, was a tough one. It was even more challenging to traverse being that I was in a new place with new teammates and living with a new family. This was my first experience in understanding how real mental health challenges can be, and I began to really get to know myself. I had to learn to open up and ask for help. It took me years to master this one but learning the mental side of the game all began in juniors.

7. HOW TO BE DISCIPLINED

In juniors, I had to learn discipline very quickly. Because there are so many elite players, coaches typically don't put up with irresponsible players. I was expected to be a true professional on and off the ice—no excuses. Either I was going to be on time and prepared for team activities, or I wasn't going to play.

For the first time in my career, I was treated like an adult. Parents calling the coaches about their child's playing time was no longer acceptable. Everything was on me now: I had to perform, or my career could've been over. Coaches didn't necessarily care how I did it as long as I delivered. General managers or coaches will simply move on to the next one up if players aren't cutting it. That's all that mattered—if the team won games and players advanced, coaches and general managers kept their jobs; if not, they were back on the job market. So, I had to perform. No one was there to tell me what to do or to remind me to work hard. A large component of high performance comes from discipline. I thought I was disciplined before, but the discipline required in juniors was much higher than I had anticipated.

8. HOW TO WORK WITH ALL DIFFERENT WALKS OF LIFE

I loved growing up in Chelsea, but I wasn't exposed to many other worldviews. My school and community were not diverse, and I was used to "living in the Chelsea bubble." I didn't really understand what that meant until I left home.

Juniors taught me that people from different backgrounds have a lot to offer, and they may view things in a different light than I do. I had to learn how to work with these different individuals and see the way they walk through life. I'd get frustrated sometimes if I didn't agree with someone, but we had to win—we always had our shared goal, so I was forced to figure out how to work towards it with everyone, no matter how different we were.

Whether it was a coaching decision I didn't like or a player's habits, I had to learn to communicate to balance differences in opinion. Being an effective team member was an important skill I had to develop.

9. HOW TO BE CONFIDENT, BUT NOT COCKY

Being from a small town in the Midwest, one of the biggest lessons I learned, ingrained in me by my family and my surrounding community since the day I was born, was to always be humble. I took that lesson to heart. I knew that if I ever achieved my dreams, I wanted to always remember where I came from—that it took a lot of help from others to get me there, along with a little luck.

While I still live by this thought process, I sometimes took it to the extreme in juniors. I would avoid talking about myself. If I ever started to feel "too good" about my play on the ice, I would actively produce thoughts that took away from my confidence to remain "even-keeled." Never too high or too low, right?

I recognize the importance of remaining humble, and I was sincerely focused on it as a young hockey player—I was so afraid someone would view me as cocky it hindered my development. I rarely took the time to build unshakable confidence in myself. I was forced to learn the line between confidence and cockiness, and sometimes to teeter on the edge of it. If I wanted to perform well, I had to. It was through pushing myself outside of my comfort zone and learning self-assuredness that I became both the hockey player and person I wanted to be.

10. HOW TO ACCEPT MY MISTAKES

When I committed to play for Harvard, my coach commented in an article about me that, "He's the model player. He works hard in the weight room, his nutrition is perfect—other players would even joke about him because Derek does everything right."

My siblings used to chirp me all the time on a similar note. After all, I was the star of the hockey team from a cozy little town who got good grades, ate healthy, didn't drink alcohol or do drugs, had a nice family, and tried my best to be a good person. When I graduated high school in 2016, the student population was 865. If you're from a small town, then you know this next sentence better than anyone: people in small towns know when someone in their community makes a mistake. I felt that pressure immensely.

I wanted to uphold that "perfect person" ideal as much as possible—I felt like I had to. I drew my growing confidence from it as a person, and it trickled into my play on the ice. I was the good guy who did things right. If I made mistakes, who was I anymore? One of the biggest assets a goalie has is their confidence. I was afraid to admit I was wrong or made mistakes because I thought I had to maintain that assurance by being right as much as possible.

I can now say I have made and will continue to make a lot of mistakes, both big and small, on and off the ice. And that's OK. It took me a long time to be able to admit this, and I have juniors to thank for helping me.

Juniors helped me learn not just this lesson but the nine others in this chapter, and plenty more. With everything juniors is to me—good, bad, and ugly—I'm grateful I got to be a part of it. Going into those leagues, all I wanted was to play in college and maybe in The League one day. While I wasn't able to play in the NHL, the real wins I took home with me are the stories, memories, and life lessons, and I wouldn't trade those for the world.

ACKNOWLEDGEMENTS

Thank you to my family Cindy, Ed, Ashley, Dave, Josh, Olivia, Jaydon, and Carter for their love and support not just in this writing process but also in life both on and off the ice over the years.

I'd also like to thank the junior league staffs, commissioners, general managers, and coaches who helped provide information about their leagues.

To my coaches throughout my life at the Chelsea Bulldogs, the Jackson Generals, the Ann Arbor Wolves, Victory Honda, the Janesville Jets, the Chicago Steel, the Lincoln Stars, and Harvard University, thank you for caring about me as a player and a person and for helping me achieve my hockey dreams.

Thank you to my high school English teacher, John Zainea, for sparking my passion to write and for encouraging me to do so.

Thank you to everyone at the Harvard Crimson Sports section, especially Amir Mamdani, for helping me develop my writing ability over the years.

Thank you to the best photographer in Lincoln, Nebraska, Brandon Anderson, for providing the photos for the cover of the book and helping grow the Lincoln stars fanbase while making us players look good.

Thank you to the people who helped with the publishing process: Amanda Karby, Veronica Scott, and Sharon AvRutick.

Finally, thank you to those who mentored me in the writing process. Jeff Adams, Evan F. Moore, Jashvina Shah, and Brian Daccord. Without your guidance, I could not have made this book a reality.

BIBLIOGRAPHY

Alberta Junior Hockey League. "AJHL History."
    https://www.ajhl.ca/ajhl-history.

Benjamin, Amalie. "Predators Prospect Prokop Comes out as Gay,
    Makes NHL History." NHL.com, July 19, 2021.
    https://www.nhl.com/news/
    nashville-prospect-luke-prokop-comes-out-as-
    gay/c-325686490.

Branch, "Derek Boogaard: A Brain 'Going Bad'." *The New York Times,*
    December 5, 2011.
    https://www.nytimes.com/2011/12/06/sports/hockey/
    derek-boogaard-a-brain-going-bad.html.

Branch, John. "Derek Boogaard: A Boy Learns to Brawl," *The New York
    Times,* December 3, 2011.
    https://www.nytimes.com/2011/12/04/sports/hockey/
    derek-boogaard-a-boy-learns-to-brawl.html.

Branch, John. "Junior Leagues Ponder Banning Hockey Fights;"
    "Rules to Be Stiffened;" "'Our Ultimate Goal Is to Remove
    Fighting,' Hockey Canada Says." *National Post,* February 29,
    2012.

British Columbia Junior Hockey League. "BCHL History."
    https://bchl.ca/bchl-history.

Bukala, Jason. "Scout's Analysis: Comparing How Leagues around the World Develop NHL Prospects." Sportsnet. October 19, 2022. https://www.sportsnet.ca/nhl/scouts-analysis-comparing-how-leagues-around-the-world-develop-nhl-prospects/.

Burke, Ashley. "Crisis on Ice: What You Need to Know about the Hockey Canada Scandal." CBC, July 29, 2022. https://www.cbc.ca/news/politics/hockey-canada-sexual-assault-crisis-parliamentary-committee-1.6535248.

Caples, Michael. "USHL Announces Rule Changes for 2017–18 Season," MiHockey. January 24, 2017, http://mihockey.com/2017/01/ushl-announces-rule-changes-for-2017-18-season/.

Central Canada Hockey League. "About the CCHL." https://www.thecchl.ca/about-the-cchl.

College Hockey Inc. "Important Answers on Family Advisors." February 5, 2013. https://collegehockeyinc.com/articles/2013/02/important-answers-family-advisors.php.

Eastern Hockey League. "All-Time EHL Records." https://www.easternhockeyleague.org/ehl-records.

——. "EHL Teams."

https://www.easternhockeyleague.org/ehl.

Griffin, Jill. "Luck Is What Happens When Preparation Meets Opportunity." *Forbes*. April 9, 2019. https://www.forbes.com/sites/jillgriffin/2019/04/09/luck-is-what-happens-when-preparation-meets-opportunity/.

Hockey Canada, "Hockey Canada Development Programs and Resources." https://www.hockeycanada.ca/en-ca/hockey-programs.

Hockey DB.com. "BCHL 2018–19 Team Attendance." https://www.hockeydb.com/nhl-attendance/att_graph_season.php?lid=BCHL2001&sid=2019.

———. "AJHL 2017–18 Team Attendance." https://www.hockeydb.com/nhl-attendance/att_graph_season.php?lid=AJHL1999&sid=2018.

———. "CCHL 2018–19 Team Attendance." https://www.hockeydb.com/nhl-attendance/att_graph_season.php?lid=CCHL2011&sid=2019.

———. "MJHL 2018–19 Team Attendance."

———. "MJHL 2018–19 Team Attendance." https://www.hockeydb.com/nhl-attendance/att_graph_season.php?lid=MJHL1999&sid=2019.

———. "NAHL 2018–19 Team Attendance." https://www.hockeydb.com/nhl-attendance/att_graph_

season.php?lid=NAHL1999&sid=2019.

———. "NOJHL 2018–19 Team Attendance."
https://www.hockeydb.com/nhl-attendance/att_graph_
season.php?lid=NOJHL1962&sid=2019.

———. "OHL 2018–19 Team Attendance."
https://www.hockeydb.com/nhl-attendance/att_graph_
season.php?lid=OHL1989&sid=2019.

———. "OJHL 2018–19 Team Attendance."
https://www.hockeydb.com/nhl-attendance/att_graph_
season.php?lid=OJHL2009&sid=2019.

———. "Ontario Hockey League [1892–2023] History and Statistics."
https://www.hockeydb.com/ihdb/stats/leagues/167.html.

———. "Ontario Junior Hockey League History and Statistics."
https://www.hockeydb.com/ihdb/stats/leagues/175.html.

———. "QMJHL 2018–19 Team Attendance."
https://www.hockeydb.com/nhl-attendance/att_graph_
season.php?lid=QMJHL1970&sid=2019.

———. "SIJHL 2018–19 Team Attendance."

———. "SIJHL 2018–19 Team Attendance."
https://www.hockeydb.com/nhl-attendance/att_graph_
season.php?lid=SIJHL2001&sid=2019.

———. "USHL 2018–19 Team Attendance."
https://www.hockeydb.com/nhl-attendance/att_graph_
season.php?lid=USHL1999&sid=2019.

——— . "WHL 2018–19 Team Attendance."

    https://www.hockeydb.com/nhl-attendance/att_graph_

    season.php?lid=WHL1979&sid=2019.

Janesville Jets Goalie Statistics.

    https://www.janesvillejets.com/stats/player-stats/

    all-teams/271?playertype=goalie.

Bromberg, Lila, "Hockey's Lack of Diversity Ingrained across the

    Sport," *Yahoo!*, September 29, 2020,

    https://www.yahoo.com/now/the-privilege-of-play-

    hockeys-racist-and-affluent-culture-still-hasnt-

    changed-140255916.html.

Lombardi, Vince. *The Essential Vince Lombardi: Words & Wisdom to*

    Motivate, Inspire, and Win (New York: McGraw Hill, 2002), 77.

Lyttle, Mason. "Schaedig, Novak Placed on NHL Central Scouting."

    October 4, 2016.

    https://www.janesvillejets.com/

    schaedig-novak-placed-on-nhl-central-scouting.

Manitoba Junior Hockey League. "MJHL History."

    https://www.mjhlhockey.ca/history.

Maritime Junior Hockey League. "History of the MHL." Accessed

    February 4, 2023,

    https://www.themhl.ca/history-of-the-mhl.

——— . "MHL League Directory."

    https://www.themhl.ca/league-directory.

Michigan High School Athletic Association, "MHSAA Ice Hockey."
https://www.mhsaa.com/sports/ice-hockey.

Moore, Evan F. and Jashvina Shah, *Game Misconduct: Hockey's Toxic Culture and How to Fix It* (Chicago: Triumph Books, 2021).

National College Athletics Association. "Men's Ice Hockey: Probability of Competing beyond High School." NCAA.org, April 20, 2020.
https://www.ncaa.org/sports/2015/3/6/men-s-ice-hockey-probability-of-competing-beyond-high-school.aspx.

North American Hockey League. "NAHL History."
http://nahl.com/history/nahl-history/index.cfm.

North American Tier III Hockey League (NA3HL). "About."
http://na3hl.com/the-na3hl/about.cfm.

———. "NA3HL Game Center 2018–19 Fan Attendance."
http://na3hl.com/game-center/#attendance?season1=169&season2=289&groupByDiv=false&gamesPlayed.

———. "Teams." http://na3hl.com/teams/.

Northern Ontario Junior Hockey League. "About the NOJHL."
https://nojhl.com/about-the-nojhl.

Ontario Hockey League. "Teams – Ontario Hockey League."
https://ontariohockeyleague.com/teamrosters/.

Paul, Rodney J. "Variations in NHL Attendance: The Impact of Violence, Scoring, and Regional Rivalries." *The American Journal of Economics and Sociology* 62, no. 2 (2003): 345–64.

https://doi.org/10.1111/1536-7150.00216.

Pointstreak Sports Technologies. "Eastern Hockey League 2014–15
Fan Attendance." http://www.pointstreak.com/prostats/
attendance.html?leagueid=1418&seasonid=12870.

———. "Home of the OJHL." http://pointstreaksites.com/view/ojhl.

Popkin, Charles A. "Ban Fighting in the NHL." *The Boston* Globe,
November 24, 2022.
https://www.bostonglobe.com/2022/11/24/opinion/
ban-fighting-nhl/.

Quebec Major Junior Hockey League. "History of the League."
https://theqmjhl.ca/history-of-the-league/.

———. "LHJMQ Standings."
https://theqmjhl.ca/standings/202/conference/.

Repke, Kristyn. "NHL Draft 101: Rules and Information." NHL.com.
June 29, 2013.
https://www.nhl.com/bluejackets/news/
nhl-draft-101-rules-and-information/c-675546.

Saskatchewan Junior Hockey League. "SJHL Historical Statistics."
https://www.sjhl.ca/historical-statistics.

———. "SJHL League Directory."
https://www.sjhl.ca/league-directory.

Superior International Junior Hockey League. "SIJHL History."
https://sijhlhockey.com/history/.

———. "SIJHL Member Clubs."

https://sijhlhockey.com/teams/.

The Junior Hockey News. "USPHL Denied Tier II Status By USA Hockey Junior Council – And What's Next," December 5, 2016, https://thejuniorhockeynews.com/usphl-denied-tier-ii-status-by-usa-hockey-junior-council-and-whats-next/.

Gulitti, Tom, "NHL Releases 2022–23 Regular-Season Schedule." NHL.com, July 6, 2022. https://www.nhl.com/news/nhl-releases-2022-23-regular-season-schedule/c-334820504.

Tyler, GC. "Understanding Junior Hockey: The Path to the NHL." https://goaliecoaches.com/understanding-junior-hockey-path-nhl/.

U.S. Census Bureau. "QuickFacts: Chelsea city, Michigan." https://www.census.gov/quickfacts/fact/table/chelseacitymichigan/HSG445221.

———. "QuickFacts: Janesville city, Wisconsin." https://www.census.gov/quickfacts/janesvillecitywisconsin.

U.S. College Hockey Online. "About Division I Men's NCAA Hockey." https://www.uscho.com/faq/about-ncaa-hockey/.

———. "Men's Division I PairWise Rankings."

https://www.uscho.com/rankings/
pairwise-rankings/d-i-men/.

United States Hockey League. "USHL Announces 2022–23
Schedule." June 21, 2022.
https://ushl.com/news/2022/8/31/ushl-announces-2022-
23-schedule.aspx.

——. "Clark Cup."
https://ushl.com/sports/2022/9/1/clarkcup.aspx.

United States Premier Hockey League. "About/History of the
USPHL."
https://www.usphlncdc.com/about-history.

USA Hockey. "USA Hockey Safe Sport Program."
https://www.usahockey.com/safesportprogram.

Western Hockey League. "About the WHL."
https://whl.ca/about.

——. "WHL Teams & Directory – WHL Network."
https://whl.ca/whl-teams-directory.

Young, Scott. *100 Years of Dropping the Puck: A History of the OHA*
(Toronto: McClelland & Stewart, 1989).